Gender in the Fiction of George Sand

FAUX TITRE

Etudes
de langue et littérature françaises
publiées

sous la direction de Keith Busby,
M.J. Freeman, Sjef Houppermans,
Paul Pelckmans et Co Vet

No. 175

Amsterdam - Atlanta, GA 2000

Gender in the Fiction
of George Sand

Françoise Massardier-Kenney

♾ The paper on which this book is printed meets the requirements of "ISO 9706:1994, Information and documentation - Paper for documents - Requirements for permanence".

♾ Le papier sur lequel le présent ouvrage est imprimé remplit les prescriptions de "ISO 9706:1994, Information et documentation - Papier pour documents - Prescriptions pour la permanence".

ISBN: 90-420-0707-9
©Editions Rodopi B.V., Amsterdam - Atlanta, GA 2000
Printed in The Netherlands

For Bill and Mélanie

ACKNOWLEDGMENTS

This project could not have been carried out without the pioneering work of Isabelle Hoog Naginski who demonstrated with *George Sand: Writing For her Life* that Sand was indeed a major writer whose works needed to be studied seriously. Nor could it have been possible without her generosity and encouragement throughout the last few years. I also wish to thank Elspeth Pope for her generous proofreading help; and the Office of Research and Graduate Studies at Kent State University for its support of the project. Finally, I could not have finished this book without the encouragement and advice of Doris Kadish; and of William Howland Kenney who not only provided insightful editing comments, but gave me steadfast moral and intellectual support .

Hudson, September 1999

CONTENTS

INTRODUCTION

Although George Sand (1804-1876) was considered one of the more significant writers in nineteenth-century France and, with Germaine de Staël, one of the leading women writers of that period, her works have for many years languished in obscurity. Fairly recently thanks to a new interest in women writing and a reconsideration of works excluded from the canon of French literature, literary scholarship has seen a surge of interest in her persona and a reexamination of her works. Until that time her name remained associated either with children's tales of pastoral life[1], or with the image of a cigar-smoking woman whose lovers and friends included major artists and thinkers of her time. Her rehabilitation as a major author is reflected in the number of scholarly and popular works that have come out in the last twenty years.

Popular recognition has ranged from additions to the many biographies such as Huguette Bouchardeau's *La lune et les sabots* (1990), Jean Chalon's *Chère George Sand* (1991), Pierre Salomon's *Née romancière* (1993), to name the most popular ones, to James Papine's movie *Impromptu* (1990), a British film that was distributed in the US and subsequently showed on PBS, to established French singer-composer Catherine Lara's rock opera *Sand et les romantiques* (1991), to a lead article in the Smithsonian magazine (Dec. 96). This mass media representation of George Sand may be unusual for a nineteenth-century author (one cannot readily imagine a rock opera based on Flaubert's life, or a best selling biography of Baudelaire), but it is a useful reminder that Sand's original appeal reached the general public, which at that time meant many women since they were the primary readers of novels[2]. It is also a reminder of Sand's crucial position in French culture as a locus where political, social, and sexual uncertainties converged. [3]

As the annual bibliography of Sand's works suggests as well, interest in her works has been reflected in the increasing number of studies that include chapters on her (see Miller (1988), Planté (1989), Kadish (1991), Macherey (1991), Reid (1993), Lukacher (1994), Ender (1995), Bergman-Carton (1995), among many others), the many articles focusing on her works, the monumental 25 volume edition of her correspondance by Georges Lubin, the two journals devoted to her *Bulletin des amis de George Sand*, and *George Sand Studies*, the reedition of her novels in a scholarly format with the Glénat press, volumes of conference proceedings, and an increasing number of translations and retranslations of her works into English.[4]

A few monographs analyzing specific aspects of Sand's works have appeared as well. The first major study to analyze Sand's works rather than her life was Kristina Wingard Vareille's *Socialité, sexualité et les impasses de l'histoire: l'évolution de la thématique sandienne d'Indiana à Mauprat* (1987) in which she showed that Sand's social ideas were formed well before she came under the influence of the two socialist male thinkers Pierre Leroux and Lammenais who are usually credited with directly influencing her works. Vareille stresses as well the thematic importance of sexuality in Sand's early works and attempts to explain Sand's lack of support of early "feminist" movements by referring to her "fémininité mythique." Wingard's study contributed to show Sand's originality and the importance of "sexualité" in the early works. But Wingard's study considers only the novels written up to 1837 whereas most of Sand's works were written afterwards, until her last work appeared on 1872.

Next, Isabelle Naginski's seminal work on Sand (1993) definitely broke away from the predominantly biographical approach that had characterized studies of Sand. She set out to demonstrate Sand's accomplishments as a major nineteenth-century writer, and her influence on the development of the novel. Naginski traces the development of Sand's "androgyny"[5] as "the fundamental basis upon which she constructed her fictional universe" (238) and argues that Sand's adoption of male attire and of a male name allowed her "to preserve her native female sympathy for traditional feminine preoccupations and values" (26). Naginski convincingly argues that by combining both masculine and feminine elements, Sand's use of narrators who are sympathetic to the plight of female characters created a "multi voiced nonhierarchical dialogue" (28). To study the development of Sand's voice, Naginski analyzed works from the 1830s and the 1840s (from *Histoire du rêveur, Indiana, Valentine, Lélia, Spiridion, Consuelo,* and *La comtesse de Rudolstadt*), works that express different sensibilities. Naginski also points out that Sand's immense literary output—eighty novels, numerous plays, autobiographical texts, articles, and twenty-five volumes of correspondance—was dismissed as evidence of mediocrity whereas her male counterparts' productivity was praised as potency. Naginski argues that Sand's immense talent for improvisation was accompanied by an incredible capacity for work[6] and that it is time she be taken seriously.

Naginski's pioneering comments on the devaluation of Sand and the importance of idealism in her works have been pursued by Naomi Schor in her book of essays *George Sand and Idealism* (1993). Schor distances herself from the lowly regular "Sandistes" (mostly women, according to Schor, whose devotion to Sand is linked to Sand's working out of "themes they hold dear-the woman artist-messiah, music, Venice, grottos, initiation, the search for the mother..."(215). Moreover, her study of the devalorization of idealism as a feminine mode is followed by a postword in which Schor comments on her lack of pleasure at reading certain of Sand's novels. However, the very fact that a prominent feminist scholar like Schor uses Sand to study the devalorization of idealism as a feminine mode is significant and ipso facto places Sand into the fold of canonic, or at least, "canonizable," authors.

   These first studies have pointed the way to crucial aspects of Sand's works. Naginski has pointed out the importance of androgyny and of idealism in Sand, while Schor has proposed a critical rethinking of idealism as "the ability of an ideal to empower and to mobilize the disenfranchised" (14). These two aspects of Sand's work: empowering the disenfranchised and the blurring of clear gender identities are crucial for understanding, not the disengagement that some academics may have felt about Sand, but the appeal that Sand has had, and continues to have on her readers. Ironically, Sand's own critique of the nineteenth-century sacralization of Art with a capital A has contributed to the lack of scrutiny of her works. The question of gender, which is crucial for an understanding of Sand's achievement and modernity has been treated at the psycho-biographical level (her dressing like a man, her pen name, her fetishism, her refusal to endorse early feminist groups, her affairs and friendships with famous artists and thinkers, etc) rather than studied in her novels.[7]

   In this study of Sand's fictional works, my goal is to show that Sand's novels were the site where she articulated a complex and extremely modern conception of gender, and where she questioned the prevalent patriarchal modes of discourse of the times, and definitions of masculinity and femininity. Sand's novels reveal a conception of gender that is increasingly contextual, a conception that has been recently articulated by Linda Alcoff and which she terms a "positional definition"[8], (i.e., what gender studies scholars call "constructivist") a non-essentializing one, and that her working out of gender positions in her fiction has an empowering effect on her readers.

Of course, the very notion of gender is now undergoing intense scrutiny in American and European feminist circles. First, as Rosi Braidotti, among others, has pointed out, "the notion of gender is a vicissitude of the English language, one which bears little or no relevance to theoretical traditions in the Romance Languages" (*Differences*: 36). However, the term does bear direct relevance to American contemporary critical discourse and whole fields of study have blossomed in a number of disciplines around the notion of gender, even if in France, for instance, nineteenth-century literature scholars still view with unease an approach that focuses on the representation of the unequal relations of men with women.

Secondly, "gender" is attacked for privileging cultural and social factors and for removing "sexual differences" from the field of feminist inquiries. Theoreticians of sexual difference like Braidotti or Judith Butler in particular argue that the sex/gender distinction reinstates a biology/culture dualism and thus reessentializes "sex" as if "sexual differences" were simply innate biological determinants. They also claim that the use of the notion of gender, which suggests a symmetry in the way men and women are constituted, obfuscates the reality of male dominance. Further, Braidotti argues that the term gender[9] fails to address the specificity of "female corpor(e)ality", i.e., a body that is conceived neither on the side of the biological nor "confined to social conditioning." Rather, still according to Braidotti, the body should be conceived as a "field of intersection of material and symbolic forces. The body is not an essence, and therefore not an anatomical destiny; it is one's primary location in the world, one's primary situation in reality." (*Patterns of Dissonance* 219) However, I would argue that the notion of "gender" does not evacuate the notion of body just described by Braidotti, nor does it necessarily entail binary or opposite terms along the nature /culture divide, as Butler argues. As gender studies sociologists Candace West and S. Fenstermaker have pointed out, "sex is socially and culturally constructed rather than a straightforward statement of the biological facts." (20). Thus I use gender as a category (like "class" or "race") that allows us to bracket preconceptions of "essence" in order to investigate notions of maleness/femaleness, femininity/masculinity as extremely complex sets of physical, symbolic, and cultural forces, and to investigate the relative importance of such forces in the definition of specific identities. Using "gender" as a category does not necessarily ignore "male dominance" (actually the term gender has developed along an awareness of male dominance) anymore than paying attention to "race" or "racialization" misses the point about white dominance. What "gender" does fail to do is to privilege the notion of "body" as the major focus in defining the identity of women. Moreover, as Gayle Rubin and Eve Sedgwick, among others, have pointed out, although sex and gender are inextricably linked, they still are not the same; in several respects, sexuality is tied more to race and class than to gender. Last, I argue that focusing on gender does not necessarily presuppose a (theoretically incorrect) notion of a unified female identity. In her discussion of the tensions between feminist theory and feminist criticism, Nina Baym has shown that the study of the images of women in literature still has much to teach us if it is done with a conscious effort to avoid universalizing claims, which is what needs to be done when analyzing a writer like Sand who thrives on crossing class and gender lines.

Actually, Sand's fictional representations of women and of the differences between the sexes prefigure the current debate in gender studies or feminist studies, a debate, as we have seen, that problematizes the very notion of gender as a stable and universal category. Her works embody the tensions expressed in contemporary feminist theory between affirmations of the existence of some essential feminine corporeality and of a feminine writing, and the view that women are a disenfranchised group whose exclusion results from specific historical and social contexts[10]. Sand's exploration of femininity is instructive because it both presents a positive conception of certain kinds of femininity (it does valorize women as women, which presupposes the existence of a common ground, if not of a feminine nature), and it puts into question the very notion of a universal femininity by suggesting that it is a male construction of subjectivity that has been internalized by most women and that needs to be rejected if these women are to become empowered. In that, she differs sharply from other French nineteenth-century women authors who, as Christine Planté has showed, internalized the very moral and cultural norms that should have prevented them from writing and expressed tremendous guilt in their writings (Planté: 151).

Examples of Sand's very complex reflection on what it means to be a woman occur very early in her life; she recounts in her autobiography *Histoire de ma vie* her revolt against the moral inferiority attributed to women and her reaction to this:

> Mais cela est faux! m'écriais-je; cette ineptie et cette frivolité que vous nous jetez à la figure, c'est le résultat de la mauvaise éducation à laquelle vous nous avez condamnées...
> Puis, m'interrogeant moi-même et me rendant bien compte des alternatives de langueur et d'énergie, c'est-à-dire de l'irrégularité de mon organisation essentiellement féminine, je voyais bien qu'une éducation rendue un peu différente de celle des autres femmes par des circonstances fortuites avait modifié mon être; que mes petits os s'étaient endurcis à la fatigue, ou bien que ma volonté développée par les théories stoïciennes de Deschartres d'une part et les mortifications chrétiennes de l'autre, s'était habituée à dominer souvent les défaillances de la nature. Je sentais bien aussi que la stupide vanité des parures, pas plus que l'impur désir de plaire à tous les hommes, n'avaient de prise sur mon esprit, formé au mépris de ces choses...Je n'étais donc pas tout à fait une femme comme celles que censurent et raillent les moralistes; j'avais dans l'âme l'enthousiasme du beau, la soif du vrai, et pourtant j'étais bien une femme comme toutes les autres, souffreteuse, nerveuse, dominée par l'imagination, puérilement accessible aux attendrissements et aux inquiétudes de la maternité...Que la femme soit différente de l'homme, que le coeur et l'esprit aient un sexe, je n'en doute pas...la femme sera toujours plus artiste et plus poète dans sa vie, l'homme le sera toujours plus dans son oeuvre (II:126-27). [11]

"But that is false," I would protest to myself. "This ineptitude and frivolity that you throw up to us is the result of the bad education to which you have condemned us...Then, questioning myself and taking stock of the alternations between languor and energy, that is to say the irregularity of my essentially feminine constitution, I saw clearly that an education somewhat different from that of other women, due to fortuitous circumstances, had modified me; that my small bones had been hardened by fatigue, or else that my will, developed by the Stoic theories of Deschartres on one hand, and Christian mortification on the other, had grown accustomed to compensate for limits set by nature. I also felt that the stupid vanity of adornment, as well as the suspect desire to please all men, had no hold on my mind, schooled to scorn them by the lessons and example of my grandmother. Therefore, I was not a woman completely like those whom some moralists censure and mock; I had in my soul an enthusiasm for the beautiful, a thirst for the true; and yet I was a woman like others-needy, nervous, prey to my imagination, childishly susceptible to the emotions and worries of being a mother....[12] That woman may differ from man, that the heart and mind answer to a sex, I do not doubt....woman will always be more artistic and poetic in her life; man will always be more so in his work" (*Story of My Life*: 899).

Sand first argues that many of the typical defects or weaknesses attributed to women (physical weakness, vanity, desire to please men) are theirs because of their lack of education. The only core characteristic left in her analysis of what constitutes a woman is maternity and the anxieties associated with it. Revealingly Sand does not mention the expected "maternal instinct." Instead of focusing on the patriarchal notion of maternity as a female biological aspect and as a social cement, she mentions a psychological (i. e., non-instinctual and non institutional) aspect. While it may seem that the adjectives used to describe these feminine characteristics reinscribe an essentialist and patriarchal definition of the feminine, a closer look shows that when Sand describes that core of the feminine, she is still contextualizing it. In her description of her

"organisation essentiellement féminine," the adjective "souffreteuse"
[handwritten annotation above "souffreteuse": *needy*]
refers to a state resulting from specific circumstances rather than from an
unavoidable state since it means either destitute, needy or sickly, half-
starved. Similarly "nervous, dominated by my imagination, childishly
susceptible to the emotions and the worries of being a mother" all refer to
Sand's situation as a mother, rather than to any of the characteristics usually
associated with femininity or maternity. After the birth of her son Maurice,
she suffered from a severe post-partum depression followed by separation
anxiety, which explains that nervousness and anxiety are presented as the
results of maternity, of a specific maternal situation. Sand's generalization
about her nature and the nature of women clearly refers to a specific
context, that of her own particular experience with the birth of her first
child; and that experience ("her primary experience in reality," to quote
Braidotti), contradicts patriarchal representations and glorification of
motherhood. What is left then of Sand's description of femininity is
ironically the dominance of imagination, a statement to which she returns
in the next paragraph. There femininity is reduced to the fact that woman's
creativity is expressed in life whereas man's creativity is expressed in his
work. While this statement does describe differences between the sexes,
it does not impute the difference in spheres of activity (private versus
public spheres) to any transcendent necessity. Moreover, it inscribes at the
heart of being a woman the ability to be an artist or a poet, which are the
very things men claimed women could not be because of their lack of
cerebral power. Thus, very early in her career, when Sand seems to
articulate her view of gender differences, she is, in fact, deconstructing
traditional definitions of gender. Furthermore when she concedes a major
difference—in this case, the role of imagination—her own activity as a
woman writer undermines the claim she makes about the universality of
this difference. In the end, giving birth with its ensuing "anxieties and
nervousness" is the only element left in Sand's discussion of femininity,
and, at that, it blurs the distinctions between the corporeal and the
psychological and it is clearly framed as an extension of her personal

experience.

Her novels are a restatement of this beginning deconstruction of gender differences and her rejection of a hierarchical binary opposition between men and women.[13] Although, in her introduction to the translation of Sand's autobiography , Thelma Jurgrau notes that "a complex set of associations with being female had promoted an ambivalence in Sand regarding her alliance to her sex" (14) and that Sand exhibits a number of gender shifts (that is, allegiances that shift from the feminine to the masculine), the previous discussion makes clear that Sand cannot exhibit any allegiance to her own "sex" since she has showed that the definition of femininity rests on negative characteristics resulting from societal constraints and that the only aspect of femininity that is directly related to the female body is maternity and its negative correlation, what she calls "excitation maladive" (V:vi: 224).

In her life, as a number of critics have pointed out, Sand did not value the company of women as women[14] and she refused to be part of early feminist militant groups. But her lack of solidarity of action with other women should not surprise us since her status as a "femme exceptionnelle" meant that she had no need to remain boxed in the category woman. As Christine Planté has reminded us, why should Sand feel the obligation to express herself as a woman (and thus to associate with women's groups) and to claim a femininity that only reflects the construction of the gaze of the Other, of Man? Sand's distance from her "own sex" is explained by her very rejection of traditional, patriarchal restrictions on what a woman had to be and by her association of most women she knows with a concept of femininity that has been male defined.[15]

However, if we move away from Sand's life and from her autobiography to examine a representative sample of her fictional works, we find a cluster of themes and strategies that consistently address the desires of female readers or women-identified readers to find representations of women that challenge essentializing negative definitions of women and that undermine traditional valorizing conceptions of masculinity. Sand questions definitions of gender by means of three major strategies: valorization of women characters as individuals, destabilization of male narrative authority, and deconstruction of female internalization of Romantic male definition of women and love.

These strategies are at play at different moments in Sand's works and they may operate singly or together, although analysis allows us to separate them. Specific novels present striking examples of these strategies and I have selected novels on the basis of their importance in the Sand canon and of their being significant examples of these empowering strategies. Chapter I analyzes Sand's valorization of victimized women characters in early novels such as *Indiana* (1832), *Jacques* (1834) and shows the limits of this valorization. Chapter II explores Sand's representation of women's desire (or its lack) in *La dernière Aldini* (1837), and *Jeanne* (1844). Chapter III analyzes Sand's questioning of Romantic narrative authority in terms of its consequence for her representation of women in *Horace* (1841), *Valvèdre* (1861), and *Melle la Quintinie* (1863). Chapter IV starts by examining Sand's representation of the ways in which gender identity is constructed and patriarchal law is internalized by women through the depiction of cross-dressing in *Gabriel* (1840); it follows with a study of the deconstruction of her women characters' internalization of male Romantic definitions of women and love in *Lucrezia Floriani* (1846). The last chapter concludes with an analysis of Sand's last work of fiction *Nanon* (1872) in which she represents a utopian version of the empowerment of women.

Apart from *Indiana*, studied in the first chapter, the novels I have chosen are not well known. The obvious reason is that since Sand's rediscovery is recent, scholars have tended to start with works written at the beginning of Sand's career or, in the case of *Nanon*, which is somewhat better known, at the very end. However, it is time that we start paying attention to a representative sample of Sand's production rather than limit our reading to a few now well known works. Sand wrote a number of major novels which have much to tell us in terms of her conception of gender and narrative authority. For instance, *Horace* (1841), although hardly ever studied, is probably the most important of Sand's socialist novels from the 1840s and it is a remarkable example of Sand's destabilization of male narrative authority. Similarly I have included *Valvèdre* (1861) because it is an excellent novel that is one of Sand's most interesting representations of marriage and a major attack on Romantic ideology. *Jeanne* (1844) is the focus of chapter III because Sand's first foray into the "pastoral" presents a fascinating representation of gender and class oppression, in a much more interesting if less reassuring version than the well-known (one could say too well-known) novels *La mare au diable* (1846) and *La petite Fadette* (1848). *Lucrezia Floriani* (1846) was chosen over *Consuelo* (1842) because, although it also focuses on a woman artist, it is a much more radical novel that offers both an example of the valorization of a professional woman artist and a critique of the internalization of Romantic definitions by the female character. *Gabriel* (1840) has recently been reedited and translated into English but has been ignored both by studies of Sand and by the literature on women and cross-dressing although it is one of the most powerful meditations on transvestism, sexual identity and women that nineteenth-century literature has to offer[16]. Because Sand's literary production was so extensive, discussions of her conception of gender or of her representation of women now need to be more inclusive and to focus on a representative sample of her works.

NOTES

1.One of the most famous examples of the survival of George Sand as a children literature author is that of Marcel Proust's narrator in *A la recherche du temps perdu* who mentions fondly his mother's reading *François le Champi* to him before she put him to bed.

2. For a study of readership in nineteenth-century France, see James Smith Allen, *Popular French Romanticism: Authors, Readers and Books in the Nineteenth-Century*. Syracuse: Syracuse University Press, 1981.

3. As Janis Bergman-Carton reminds us in her illuminating study of women of ideas in nineteenth-century French art, Sand was the single most represented woman in the first part of the nineteenth-century. Unlike other women authors, she controlled to a higher degree "the construction of her authorial   persona than any other woman in the period. The commission, conception, and dissemination of portraits was one of the several methods she used to elicit and imprint her persona on French culture" (207). The centrality of Sand as a cultural icon may explain why she never disappeared from popular culture while literary studies were still ignoring her. Bergman-Carton, Janis. *The Woman of Ideas in French Art.* New Haven: Yale University Press, 1995.

4.For an annual list of works on Sand, or editions and translations of her works, see my bibliography in David V. Erdman, ed *The Romantic Movement. A Selective and Critical Bibliography.* West Cornwall, Ct: Locust Hill Press.

5.Kari Weil has showed how important the figure of the androgyne was in nineteenth-century French literature and how it has primarily functioned as an ideal based on patriarchal ideology. However, her study only includes male authors; Balzac or Gauthier's treatment of androgyny could fruitfully be contrasted with that of Sand. Kari Weil. *Androgyny and the Denial of Difference.* Charlottesville: University of Virginia Press, 1992.

6. For most of her life, Sand only slept four hours per night. Henry James, always astute, has pointed out how Sand's work regimen upset her male writer friends who could not keep up.

7. Sand's handling of gender has been studied at the iconographic level by Janis Bergman-Carton (1995).

8. To go beyond the nominalist/essentialist quagmire, Alcoff suggests that "When the concept "woman" is defined not by a particular set of attributes but by a particular position, the internal characteristics of the person thus identified are not denoted so much as the external context within which that person is situated" (432). Linda Alcoff, "Cultural Feminism versus Post-Structuralism: The Identity Crisis in Feminist Theory. *Signs* 13.3 (1988): 405-36. "

9. This criticism can have validity in the specific political context of academia and academic publishing in cases where "gender" has been used to shift resources away from women studies and direct them toward "men" studies.

10. For useful discussions of conflicting views within women studies, see Evelyn Fox Keller's *Conflicts in Feminism* (1990), Nancy Fraser and Sandra Lee Bartky's *Revaluing French Feminism* (1992), and Michele Barrett and Anne Philippe's *Destabilizing Theory:*

Contemporary Feminist Debate (1992).

11. This excerpt has been often quoted but never in its entirety, so that the complexity and instability of the definitions Sand is working out do not come through.

12. I am following the group translation of *Story of My Life*, edited by Thelma Jurgrau, with some modifications when accuracy required it. Whereas the translators used "dependent" for "souffreteuse" I use "needy." I changed "the emotionalism and anxieties of motherhood" to "the emotions and the worries of being a mother" which is a more accurate and less negative rendition of "aux attendrissements et aux inquiétudes de la maternité." Thelma Jurgrau, ed. *Story of My Life*. Albany: State University of New York Press, 1991.

13. In an attempt to discredit women authors, nineteenth-century anti-feminists writers invoked the specter of hybridity. The critic Lasserre thus observed that George Sand was "de race très mêlée" (qtd in Planté: 121) but he could well have added that she was "de sexe très mêlé."

14. However, she had a number of friendships with women who tended not to be "ordinary women." Among these accomplished artists or writers were opera singer Pauline Viardot, actress Marie Dorval or writer Daniel Stern (i.e., Marie d'Agoult).

15. Actually, as the lives of a number of Saint Simonian women sadly reveal, these militant women turned out to be victimized by the men and the tenets of the very movement that purported to give them "freedom." Later in the century, even a life-long militant suffragette like Hubertine Auclert (who was a great admirer of George Sand) was rejected by other feminist groups of the times. It looks as if this modern notion of "female solidarity" to which earlier women should have subscribed need to be reexamined in light of the historical conditions of the times.

16. The only pieces dealing with *Gabriel* are two articles: Veronica Hubert-Matthews, "*Gabriel* ou la Pensée sandienne sur l'identité sexuelle." *George Sand Studies* 13 (1994): 19-28 (1994); and Ann McCall E., "George Sand and the Genealogy of Terror." *Ecriture* 34 (1995): 38-48.

CHAPTER I
VICTIMIZATION IN *INDIANA* AND *JACQUES*

George Sand's life-long investigation of the meaning of "woman"and her questioning of the hierarchical binary oppositions between men and women is evident in her first novel, the famous *Indiana* (1832) and the lesser known fine epistolary novel *Jacques* (1834). In these two works, Sand began to lay bare the cultural mechanisms responsible for gender inequalities and began a pattern of using ambiguous protagonists in order to bring attention to the incoherence of established gender positions. Sand's first novel (1832) attracted considerable attention when it was first published and is one of the few among her works to be systematically discussed by contemporary critics. In 1832, critics focused on its realism and compared it to the work of Stendhal, while recent critics have perceived it as Sand's attempt to find a literary voice separate from realism (i.e., something called "idealism"). As Sandy Petrey has demonstrated in his analysis of the critical reception of 1832, *Indiana*'s appeal at the time was a "realist" appeal whereby the novel shows that life is formed by forces that vary with time and place, and it is also the reason for its appeal now: gender is one of the "components of human existence that vary with time, place and customs" (134); and gender is interrelated with genre.[1]

However, beyond the continuity of its appeal, *Indiana* continues to give rise to opposite interpretations of what Sand's novel says about gender matters and what character is used to represent Sand's position. In *Working for Her Life*, Isabelle Naginski has argued that the novel registers Sand's new found literary voice, which is embodied by the character of Ralph[2]; whereas Marilyn Lukacher reads *Indiana* as the impossible attempt to choose between two mother figures: Sand's aristocratic grandmother and her plebeian mother and sees a parallel, not between Sand and Ralph, but between Sand and Raymon[3]. Some critics see the end of the novel where Ralph and Indiana escape to the idyllic setting of Bernica, as a flaw in a realist text[4] while others attempt to justify the ending as befitting an idealist and/or a feminist text. For instance, in his justification of the end, Nigel Harkness rereads *Indiana* as proposing an essentialist view and the end as claiming a feminist silence[5], while Petrey demonstrates that the novel is based on a constructivist notion of gender. Last, some, like Leslie Rabine, argue that Sand represents woman as passive and chaste (i.e., as reproducing a conservative nineteenth-century ideology) while others, like Kathryn Crecelius, point out that Sand shows how "religious, social, and political systems combine to oppress women" (73)[6]. Kristina Wingard Vareille also stresses the importance of Sand's critique of marriage and of the condition of women in *Indiana* but also points out that this critique is not limited to women since Sand shows that men almost as much as women are victimized by traditional marriage. [7]

These varied and sometimes contradictory interpretations stem from the novel's own contradictions and from a number of narrative shifts that prevent critical attempts to interpret it as a coherent narrative because precisely the novel's theme is the incoherence of gender positions. In *Indiana* Sand is analyzing and bringing to the surface mechanisms of victimization based on gender, race, and class and is questioning the stability of gender boundaries that buttress power inequalities through a systematic undermining of narrative authority and consistency. Although the final episode of the plot is usually the place where the disruption of the "idealist" is perceived, Sand has undermined the coherence of her own narrative well before the end through the manipulation of the omniscient narrator and through contradictory presentations of characters.

Although interpretations of *Indiana* vary greatly, there seems to be a critical consensus about the fact that the final episode of *Indiana* is an idealist happy ending. Whether critics approve of it or criticize it for its switch in mode, they consider what happens after the scene where Ralph and Indiana leap to their death a positive outcome: the protagonists don't die and live together happily ever after. However, their lives on a secluded plantation where they employ old or weak former slaves that they have freed may seem an "idealist" or "happy" solution only if readers identify with the patriarchal omniscient narrator. For this final episode obliterates the character of Indiana who becomes passive and silent[8]. The narrative is made by the male narrator for a male friend as recounted by Ralph the male protagonist who thus becomes the hero of the novel.

Indiana's transformation from a rebellious and articulate victim[9] into a sweet and languid character [according to the narrator, her eyes have a "douceur incomparable/unique sweetness" (337) and her manners have "quelque chose de lent et de triste qui est naturel aux créoles/something slow and sad that comes naturally to creole women" (337)] starts with the suicide scene where Ralph not only takes over discourse and recounts his long hidden passion for her but also directs all their actions [" il prit sa fiancée dans ses bras et l'emporta pour la précipiter avec lui dans le torrent/he took his fiancée in his arms and led her away to hurl her with him in the torrent" (330)]. The following "idyllic" episode repeats this pattern whereby Ralph controls discourse and action. When the narrator alludes to gossip concerning them among the colonists, Ralph silences him, and once Indiana is out of earshot, he accepts to tell his story "je vous dirai mon histoire, mais pas devant Indiana. Il est des blessures qu'il ne faut pas réveiller/I shall tell you my story, but not in front of Indiana. There are wounds that should not be reopened." (338) [note that he refers to it as *his* story, not hers], repeating a pattern of silence and withdrawal of information justified by the mistaken goal of protecting weak women. All of a sudden, Indiana's story has become Ralph's story and the novel ends with a dramatic shift away from the mechanisms of victimization of women to the emergence of the male Romantic hero.

While Ralph's own victimization and opposition to patriarchal structures may explain some critics' acceptance of his Romantic positioning as representing the voice of the author, his participation in those very patriarchal power structures and his final effective silencing of Indiana should warn the readers that identifying the author's position may be more difficult than the surface narrative would lead us to expect.

Ralph's surprising and seductive transformation into a passionate, articulate opponent of the debased values of Restoration society, and his endorsement by the omniscient narrator trap the readers into glossing over Indiana's erasure and, more importantly, into ignoring Sand's careful construction of Ralph as a character who participates in the victimization of women even though he is himself the victim of patriarchal law and even though, as Doris Kadish has noticed, he has been "symbolically emasculated and feminized through analogy with women, slaves, and members of oppressed groups" (27).

Sand's association of Ralph with some feminized traits, however, must be seen as part of her attempt to show that the unequal status of the two "sexes" is not based on any natural division but is a complex set of gender positions occupied by men and women who have different amounts of control over their lives. To see that Ralph is silent and submissive (i.e., positioned as a woman) does not mean that he represents the voice of the author. An examination of Ralph's history and personality reveals both his victimization and the extent of his participation in the structures that disenfranchise most women. Thus Sand's construction of Ralph is paradoxical.

Sand uses the omniscient narrator to present Ralph in a deceiving and ultimately inconsistent way. As Crecelius has noted, the presentation of Ralph gives rise to "certain inconsistencies" (77) because he is presented from the point of view of Indiana rather than in an objective way, as Sand's use of an omniscient narrator would lead the readers to expect. I would argue that the entire presentation of Ralph is suspect. The details describing Ralph given at the beginning of the novel consistently undermine the portrait made later. The Ralph of the beginning of the novel is characterized by the omniscient narrator as a well fed, dull character, an "homme dormeur et bien mangeant" (51). His features are "régulièrement fades/regularly dull" (51), his portrait in Indiana's room is insignificant and "only the original is more insignificant than the portrait" (108); still according to the narrator Indiana's and Ralph's personalities are totally incompatible (51). Moreover, Ralph is presented as a friend of Delmare, Indiana's tyrannical husband. Ralph also despises women as the narrator's description of his innermost thoughts indicate. When Ralph expresses his distrust of rhetoric as opposed to ideas (in the idealist belief, one assumes, that ideas can be evaluated separately from the language in which they are articulated), he blames women especially for paying more attention to form than to content, and for being highly susceptible to flattery. Indiana's reaction to his remarks "vous avez un profond dédain pour les femmes/you have a great disdain for women" (58) correctly interprets his comments as expressing his belief in the inferiority of women.

When Noun, Indiana's servant becomes agitated upon hearing that Delmare is out with a gun and risks wounding her secret lover Raymon de Ramière, and when Indiana also shows concern, the narrator makes us privy to Ralph's thoughts "Ces deux femmes sont folles, pensa Sir Ralph. D'ailleurs ajouta-t-il en lui-même, toutes les femmes le sont/these two women are crazy, thought Sir Ralph. Anyway, he thought on to himself, all women are" (61). He adds later "Quelles misérables terreurs de femmes/ what miserable women terrors" (62). This is the same Ralph who at the end of the novel is presented as Indiana's ideal lover and interpreted as Sand's voice.

Furthermore, the theme of women's ignorance and specifically of Indiana's ignorance is linked throughout the novel to Ralph's conception of women as intellectually deficient. When, near the end of the novel, Ralph finally tells Indiana of his passion for her and recounts his role in her life: "Je fis de vous ma soeur, ma fille, ma compagne, mon élève, ma société/I made you my sister, my daughter, my companion, my student, my community" (316), the reader may be seduced by his passionate language (his "rhetoric") and forget that it is Ralph's upbringing that has made Indiana into an ignorant person whose subsequent intellectual weakness confirms his patriarchal belief about women's innate inferiority. As the omniscient narrator had reminded the reader, Indiana had been brought up by Ralph "qui avait une médiocre opinion de l'intelligence et du raisonnement chez les femmes...Elle savait donc à peine l'histoire agrégée du monde et toute discussion sérieuse l'accablait d'ennui/ who had a poor opinion of women's intelligence and capacity for reasoning...Thus she hardly knew any world history and any serious discussion bored her to tears" (174). This reminder by the narrator about Ralph's responsibility in Indiana's lack of intellectual maturity not only contradicts the same narrator's later endorsement of Ralph but is part of the novel's insistence on the role of men's prejudice in propagating women's ignorance and then blaming them for it. Sand ties the question of women's ignorance to the mechanisms of victimization through which knowledge is withheld from disenfranchised groups, be they women, servants or slaves. Because of her class, Indiana has at least learned to read and write as her letters to Raymon indicate. However, such is not the case for her servant and friend Noun; she makes a number of spelling errors in her letter to the same Raymon, who, upon receiving her letter, decides to leave her as such lack of control of French grammar clearly marks Noun's social inferiority and reminds him of the impossibility of continuing his affair with her.

The withholding of knowledge and of information because of the male characters' belief in the inability of women to understand the information is not the sole prerogative of Ralph; it characterizes all the male characters who have some power but it indicates that Ralph participates in the reproduction of patriarchal structures that are inimical to women. Besides his denial of education to Indiana, who is his sole love and anchor, Ralph also withholds from her crucial information about Noun and Raymon. In agreement with Delmare, Ralph keeps silent about the fact that Indiana's friend and maid is having a secret affair with Raymon, and thus further isolates Noun and allows Indiana to fall prey to Raymon's schemes. Similarly, at the end of the novel, he prevents the narrator from repeating what he has heard in order to protect Indiana as if she were a child. Ralph's role in denying women access to knowledge is incompatible with interpreting him as an ideal androgynous character. On the contrary it suggests that weak and silent characters may participate in their own victimization, as we shall see with Indiana' and Noun's attitudes toward their lover.

Even the facts of Ralph's early life as recounted by Indiana suggest Ralph's acquiescence and implication in the victimization of women. Significantly, it is Indiana who tells Ralph's story, in contrast to the end of the novel where Ralph is in control of the narrative. Indiana recounts to Raymon Ralph's first unhappy years during which he is rejected by his parents who prefer his less shy and more demonstrative older brother. Ralph is so depressed by his life that he is on the verge of committing suicide by drowning in the ocean[10] when he sees his young cousin Indiana (then five years old) who runs to him and hugs him. He decides to live for her and to take care of her (158). Ralph is thus saved from despair by the love of a child. As an adolescent he takes care of the orphaned Indiana, but after his own brother's death, he is forced to marry his brother's fiancee for unspecified family reasons (the reader assumes it is a financial arrangement between the two families). Ralph leaves for England with his wife who loved his brother and abhors him; has a son, and returns to the island of Bourbon after the death of his wife and son. Raymon, to whom Indiana is recounting this story, astutely wonders why Ralph didn't marry Indiana and she invokes her lack of wealth as a reason. The narrative of Ralph's life emphasizes the necessity of having a child-like woman for the melancholy hero to survive, but also Ralph's own victimization. The novel represents the patriarchal pattern of victimization which includes women, slaves, and men who don't occupy a position of power. Ralph is the second son, rejected by his parents and forced to marry for social and financial reasons while Indiana is also ignored by her relatives and married off to a much older man. In both cases families have broken down and have lost their protective vocation. Family structure is presented as the occasion to consolidate power positions. The pervasive corruption of the traditional family in which fathers no longer protect and mothers no longer nurture indicate Sand's conviction that the oppression of the weak—children, women, men, slaves—is endemic to the Restoration society she represents and that, by the logic of their own participation in such family structures, her characters can turn oppressors too.

By agreeing to marry his dead brother's betrothed, even though he knows of her love for his brother, Ralph puts himself in the position of a Delmare. Moreover, since Ralph had a son with this woman, whereas the question of Delmare's actually consummating his marriage with Indiana is left ambiguous, the reader must assume that Ralph forced himself on his wife to produce an heir or at least that he consumed his union knowing of her repulsion. Ralph's consent to marry is explained by his unwillingness to be disowned by his father (by which one assumes he will be disinherited since he has already been rejected emotionally by his parents).

Thus his allegiance to patriarchal values and his participation in oppressive practices, and his long lasting contempt for women must not be forgotten even in the context of his being later presented as the prototypical melancholy and isolated Romantic hero of the "idyllic" end of the novel. Ironically, Ralph is the character who had claimed the superiority of actions and ideas over words, but who is absolved because of his final control of the narrative. The complexity of Ralph's role, the mix of victim and victimizer allows Sand to show the difficulty of escaping oppression as long as human beings accept binary systems of opposition whereby one category is posed as inferior to the other (women to men, slaves to masters). By luring the reader into accepting Ralph as the "idealist" solution to Indiana's fate, by carefully constructing him as the Romantic figure who finally comes to speech, Sand problematizes any notion of liberation that is not accompanied by a radical rethinking of gender and social categories. Ralph loves and saves Indiana but his adherence to paternalistic views of women condemns him to play the role of a traditional husband, one surely more palatable than the old, tyrannical Delmare, but still one which spells the end of Indiana's psychological and moral autonomy.[11]

This interiorization of patriarchal values by characters who articulate their opposition to the political or social aspects of these structures is shared by women characters as well, an idea to which Sand will return on several occasions and even more pointedly in later novels and which explains in part her reluctance to accept the category "women" as a rallying point because this very notion of woman often stands, as she demonstrates, for definitions of women articulated by and for the benefit of patriarchal subjects.

Women characters in *Indiana* follow Ralph's pattern of rebellion against the patriarchy while internalizing its norm or simply accepting and reproducing these structures if their position on the power scale allows it. Sand uses a range of women to show their implication in these oppressive practices: from a wealthy aristocrat (Laure de Nagy) to a servant who is possibly a former slave (Noun).

At one end of the power spectrum, Laure de Nagy who marries Raymon because he has the right pedigree and she can control him, occupies the position of "male" power. As Petrey has noticed, "the power granted Laure by historical changes affects nothing less than the obliteration of male hegemony" (141), but it is not so much male hegemony that is obliterated as the demonstration that gender performance has replaced notions of natural biological sexual differences to found inequalities. Laure de Nagy performs as a male. The obliteration of the power of the individual male leaves the structure intact. The character of Laure occupies a "masculine" position and thus further demonstrates the constructedness of notions of masculinity and femininity. Her social and economic position (an orphan from an old noble family who has been adopted by a rich industrialist), gives her the power to assess the desirability of potential male partners and to decide whom she will marry. Even before she becomes a major character, Sand introduces her as one of the spectators and commentators at the ball where Raymon recognizes Indiana and starts flirting with her. While Indiana innocently falls for Raymon's attentions, Laura watches him and invites gossip and information about him in a scene that inverts gender roles by placing her as the subject gazing. Laura's biological sexual identity is compensated by her social position; her gender role is that of male domination in contrast to Indiana's lower position and victimization, and later adoption of female submission. By providing these opposite examples of feminine performance, a tactic she will use as well in the novels discussed in subsequent chapters, Sand suggests that masculinity and femininity are positions that are linked to social and economic power more than to "nature" and that they could be negotiated. Sand shows that these gender inequalities are enforced through external pressures and through internal mechanisms (when individuals internalize imposed definitions and come to consider them natural, i.e., women can't think, women are weak, women are natural mothers, etc).

Whereas Laure de Nagy's mental attitude is one of extreme power, Indiana's and Noun's reflect their inferior status and their ultimate acceptance of their inferiority. The orphan Indiana, daughter of an impoverished noble family was given to a much older man (she is sixteen and he is sixty), ex-soldier turned business man whose money endeared him to her relatives, whereas Noun is a servant who follows Indiana wherever she moves. Although we are given no details (we don't know whether Noun's mother was a slave or free, or even whether Noun is black), her position as a domestic is clear and provides a more pronounced version of Indiana's own situation of servitude.

What is less evident is the importance of servitude in shaping these characters' own attitudes. Indiana may denounce the inequity of the laws that allow her husband's domination but when she leaves Bourbon to join Raymon, she can only speak in terms of abjection and servitude "c'est ton esclave que tu as rappelée de l'exil/ here is your slave that you called back from exile" (296), and "Je viens pour te donner du bonheur, pour être ce que tu voudras, ta compagne, ta servante ou ta maîtresse/I come to give you some happiness, to be what you want, your companion, your servant or your mistress" (296), "je suis ton bien, tu es mon maître/ I am your thing, you are my master" (297). Indiana's discourse, which is steeped in the vocabulary of slavery and which is a part of a pattern where relationships between men and women are described with a vocabulary of enslavement and subjection, reveals Sand's understanding of the mechanisms of subjection: the long-lasting subjection and state of ignorance in which women have been forced to live have resulted in their acceptance and internalization of the hierarchical structures that created their bondage; as a result, even when these structures of coercion are removed (i.e., when Indiana escapes from her husband), the women characters retain a mental frame that conceptualizes "love" as bondage or as a relation of inequality.

When Noun attempts to regain Raymon's favors after she finds out that she is pregnant, she rejects his offers of financial support and uses the same metaphors that Indiana would later use. She even proposes to Raymon to work as his servant (as she is already his mistress, it is the only position that she can envision). She tells him "Je ne suis pas exigeante; je n'ambitionne point ce qu'une autre à ma place aurait peut-être eu l'art d'obtenir. Mais permettez-moi d'être votre servante/I am not demanding; I don't hope for what another woman in my place would have been artful enough to obtain. But allow me to be your servant." (110). So while Noun feels insulted by Raymon's offer of money (an offer which clearly means the end of their relationship), she is ready to surrender her whole being in order to be next to him. Isabelle Naginski has remarked that Noun is almost without speech (64) but actually it is the force of her eloquence that convinces Raymon not to break up as he intended. The narrator's comment on her appeal "Noun parla longtemps ainsi. Elle ne se servit peut-être pas des mêmes mots, mais elle dit les mêmes choses, bien mieux, cent fois que je ne pourrais les redire/Noun spoke thus for a long time. She perhaps did not use exactly the same words, but she said the same things, much better, a hundred times better than I could repeat them" (102). Noun may use the language of female subjection as Naginski and others have argued, but it is an extremely articulate language that describes accurately that state of mental bondage that characterizes women who don't benefit from a social position that can counterbalance gender positions. Indiana's and Noun's statements both articulate their acceptance that what they are is defined by what the male other wants. Indiana's "Je serai ce que tu voudras/ I will be what you want" (296) echoes Noun's "Je me hais puisque je ne vous plais plus/I hate myself since I no longer please you" (102). The grammatical slip of the "what" instead of a "who" indicates the extent of Indiana's vision of herself as an object rather than as a subject, even in a situation which is the result of her will and of remarkable determination and courage.

In *Indiana*, love is thus presented as another locus for women's oppression. Not surprisingly Laure de Nagy, the only powerful woman in the novel, rejects the idea of "love" because she knows that, paradoxically, her wealth will make it impossible for her to disentangle genuine affection from ambition or greed. The ignorant and powerless Indiana and Noun who embrace romantic notions of love are destroyed by their acceptance of love as a relation that disempowers them. Whether this love includes a sexual relation or not, it is a negative experience[12]. The sexual relation just increases the chance that the woman will be victimized more quickly, as happens with Noun or with the other women that Raymon has discredited. Sexuality, like romantic love and marriage, has no positive ideological function in *Indiana*. The new order proposed at the end of the novel is very problematic as the previous analysis of its implication has shown. Although Kristina Wingard argues that Sand discretely suggests that Ralph and Indiana consummate their union[13] and that Indiana can finally accept her sexuality without danger or suffering, the final episode is curiously ambiguous about their status as a couple. This ambiguity reflects Sand's own ambiguity about the limits of the figure of Ralph as a solution. Her heroes are cut off from the external social structures of the world but they have interiorized gender roles. Thus the question of sexuality is erased[14]. Criticism of Sand for representing Indiana as a chaste *bourgeoise* fails to notice that Sand presents all the scenarios possible for a woman: marriage with sex (Laure de Nagy), love and sex (Noun), love without sex (Indiana), and that none of these scenarios can be fulfilling because of the power structure[15].

Sand's commitment to providing her readers with a constructivist conception of gender is such that the novel presents an unusual number of women who either are not mothers (thus whose lives as women contradicts traditional conceptions of "femininity" that rely on maternity as its linchpin or who as mothers or mother figures function as agents of reproduction of the social order. Sand's deconstruction of stable gender categories includes a reexamination of the roles of mothers in the reproduction of patriarchy and femininity.

First of all maternity and the ability to procreate among women of child bearing age is associated with death. Ralph's wife and his young son are dead by the beginning of the novel and, of course, Noun commits suicide while pregnant because her lover Raymon no longer wishes to carry on their affair. The other protagonists who are young women and who survive—Indiana and Laure de Nagy—are both childless and their own mothers are dead, an interesting coincidence if one recalls Sand's discussion of gender differences in which she mentions maternity as the only difference separating the sexes.[16]

The older women who are actual mothers (for instance, Raymon's mother) or who are mother substitutes (Mme de Carvajal, Indiana's aunt) are both aristocrats who are presented as opportunistic survivors of political and social upheavals or as educating their male offsprings to be victimizers.

Mme de Carjaval, who has ignored her niece, starts to show her much affection when she realizes that Delmare has become a successful businessman ("Madame de Carvajal aux yeux de qui la fortune était la première recommendation, témoigna beaucoup d'affection à sa nièce et lui promit le reste de son héritage/Madame de Carvajal who considered wealth of foremost importance, showed her niece much affection and promised her the rest of her inheritance" (86). The details of her life provided by the narrator draw the portrait of an opportunist for whom fortune and appearances are foremost: a widowed Spanish aristocrat who was an admirer of Napoleon, she has made a fortune speculating on the stock market and, according to the narrator "A force d'esprit, d'intrigues et de dévotion elle avait obtenu, en outre, les faveurs de la cour/ Through her wit, schemes, and devotion she had moreover obtained the favors of the court" (85). Mme de Carjaval uses her pretty niece Indiana to attract young fashionable men to her salon. She sees no objection to her niece's involvement with Raymon but is ready to disown her when gossip about their alleged affair threatens to break out and sully her reputation as a pious older woman. Sand's biting portrait of Mme de Carjaval as a crafty maneuverer who adopts the current ideologies (religiousness and the monarchy) and who gains power and money shows how little room there is to nurture and protect younger women like Indiana. These characters represent such disparate human types (one powerful, savvy, and independent; the other powerless, naive, and ignorant) that the fact that they are both women becomes irrelevant and cannot lead to any allegiance based on their sex.

In fact, Sand's presentation of women protagonists who belong to an older generation suggests that what these older women nurture is the reproduction of the very patriarchal structures that allow younger women without power to be bartered and exploited. An analysis of the presentation of Raymon's mother also shows the care with which Sand constructed her not as the positive character which most critics have seen, but as a very ambiguous, misguided, not to say negative, figure[17]. Sand's portrait of

Raymon's mother as a good mother is ironic since that characteristic is always invoked in the context of his mistreatment of women. When the narrator describes Raymon's desertion of the pregnant Noun, he links his action to a class prejudice "Pour lui, une grisette n'était pas une femme/ for him a *grisette* was not a woman" (75), which the narrator exonerates by commenting "Tout cela n'était pas la faute de Raymon; on [read his mother since his father has been long dead] l'avait élevé pour le monde/All this was not Raymon's fault; he had been brought up for fashionable society" (75). His mother is held responsible for his considering lower class women sub-human and not warranting the treatment reserved to "women," that is women of one's class who can provide social and financial alliances.

Thus in *Indiana*, as in the works examined in the other chapters, being a woman has a host of different meanings depending on the class to which an individual woman belongs. The higher the class, the more power she has and the less she shares with other women. The disparity of interests between younger poorer women and older aristocratic women is emphasized by Raymon's reactions to Noun after he attempts to break off with her. The omniscient narrator explains Raymon's eagerness to get rid of Noun by invoking his mother "Il en coûtait à Raymon de tromper une si bonne mère/It was difficult for Raymon to deceive such a good mother" (76).

Raymon's mother is thus directly linked to his treatment of Noun. The narrator follows with an ironically positive portrait of Raymon's mother as a woman with intellectual and moral qualities who has given him "ces excellents principes qui le ramenaient toujours au bien/ those excellent principles that always brought him back to good" (78). Since the reader was just told how Raymon avoids responsibility [that would be the "bien" to which he returns] by invoking the need to spare his mother, the principles that his mother has taught him are reduced to simple narcissism[18]. Sand thus uses the omniscient narrator to say one thing but to mean another. The positive portrait of Raymon's mother seems to be used to excuse the behavior of the son but actually serves to implicate his mother in his corruption.

The ambiguity of the role of Raymon's mother is further developed through the narrator's comments alluding to the vicissitudes of her life. She is a woman who went through "des époques si différentes que leur esprit a pris toute la souplesse de leur destinée/ such different times that their mind has adopted the suppleness of their destiny" (78). While the narrator presents this information positively, it parallels his other comments about Mme de Carjaval's ability to adapt to different moral codes, an ability, as we have seen, which is a sign of corruption. After Noun's suicide, the narrator explains that Raymon feels remorse and thinks of blowing his brains out but "un sentiment louable l'arrêta. Que deviendrait-sa mère...sa mère âgée, débile/a worthy feeling stopped him. What would become of his mother, so old and weak?" (127). Again his mother is the excuse for his failure to act.

The role of Raymon's mother as the explanation and justification for his narcissistic behavior is linked not only to Noun's fate but also to Indiana's. After Noun's suicide, Indiana refuses to see Raymon, but her husband imposes Raymon's visit on her because he has been charmed by Raymon's mother (122). Raymon in turn uses his mother to come visit Indiana who is seduced by her charm "qu'un esprit supérieur joint à une âme noble et généreuse, sait répandre dans ses moindres relations/ that a superior mind linked to a noble and generous soul can infuse in all her relationships" 140. Indiana's "fascination de coeur" with Madame de Ramière is linked to her not having known her own mother (141).

The complexity of Raymon's mother's role is further demonstrated in the episode in which Indiana compromises herself by coming to see him late at night and he attempts to make her leave by asking his mother to help. Mme de Ramière acts very generously toward Indiana but as the narrator's analysis makes clear, she has created Raymon's selfishness and self-indulgence: "Le caractère de ce fils impétueux et froid, raisonneur et passionné était une conséquense de son inépuisable amour et de sa tendresse généreuse pour lui...mais elle l'avait habitué à profiter de tous les sacrifices qu'elle consentait à lui faire...A force de générosité, elle n'avait réussi qu'à former un coeur égoïste/ The character of this impetuous and cold, reasoning and passionate son was a consequence of her unending love and her generous affection...but she had accustomed him to profit from all the sacrifices she was willing to make for him... By dint of generosity, she had only succeeded in shaping a selfish heart" (223). This analysis presents Raymon's narcissism, not as a natural "male" trait, but as the product of his mother's indulgence, that is as the product of specific cultural practices that reproduce hierarchies. Loving a son means encouraging narcissistic behavior and victimizing women. Ironically, mothers, as Sand presents them in *Indiana*, are the social agents through which gender inequalities are passed on to the next generation.

Sand's early description of the cultural mechanisms at work in the construction of gender inequalities and her reliance on highly ambiguous protagonists to suggest the complexity of oppressive practices was to find another expression two years later in *Jacques*, an epistolary novel written during her stay in Venice and published in 1834. The novel received universal negative criticisms from journalists and fellow writers because they found the story offensive: a man (Jacques) marries a younger woman without a dowry (Fernande) and attempts to have an "enlightened" marriage based on mutual respect rather than on duty. Consequently, when Fernande falls in love with a young man by the name of Octave, Jacques decides to disappear in what appears to be a mountain climbing accident in order to let her live her life. Sand's criticism of the indissolubility of marriage and her decision to sacrifice the hero in order to save the happiness of the adulterous wife ran counter to tradition[19] and offended sensibilities in so far as the husband is no Delmare figure. Jacques is presented as a superior man, an articulate and gifted former soldier mined by the *mal du siècle*, a much improved version of Ralph.

More recently, critics have identified Jacques with Sand's own position and tied Sand's pessimism to the specific circumstances in which she wrote the novel (i.e., the painful break-up with Musset in Venice).

More importantly, however, the concerns exhibited in *Indiana* resurface, and the type of the Romantic hero presented as a solution to women's victimization in *Indiana* is finally rejected. Furthermore, Sand's exploration of the constructedness of gender roles becomes more daring and her analysis of the difficulty of changing roles becomes more pointed. Also, contrary to what she did in *Indiana*, Sand creates women characters whose sexuality is not evaded, but explored in ways that reveal the anxiety it fosters. Last her representation of a variety of women characters shows even more clearly than in *Indiana* how problematic the notion of woman is.

There are four main women characters in the novel: Fernande, a sensitive young woman whom Jacques marries; her confidante and correspondent, Clémence, a young widow who has retired to a convent and who gives Fernande advice full of commonsensical cynicism; Sylvia, Jacques' ward, the illegitimate daughter of Fernande's mother, who may be Jacques half-sister as well; and finally, Mme de Theursan, the figure of the "bad mother," a former lover of Jacques's father. Since the novel consists only of letters written by characters to each other, unlike what occurred in *Indiana*, there is no narrator to guide or misguide the reader, who has to create meaning out of the different versions of events presented by these letter writers. While Mme de Theursan is at the origin of much of the plot, it is only the younger generation who speak or write and it is the women who write the most. All together the young women write 47 letters (Fernande 28, Sylvia 14, Clémence 5) while Jacques writes 26 letters and Octave, Sylvia's former lover and Fernande's own lover, writes 10. The volume of the letters written by women suggests that their private voice is paramount; by dispensing with the narrator, Sand removes the patriarchal filter that obfuscated the access to characters in *Indiana*, and by providing a multiplicity of voices and points of view, she repeats at the structural level the contradictions that she is exploring.

Sand redeploys the theme of the "bad mother" which she had begun developing in *Indiana* where mothers were either absent or where mother figures were negative, but, rather than just concentrating on the negative aspects for younger women of the mother figure as agent of the reproduction of patriarchal structures, she also suggests that Mme de Theursan is not only a bad mother; she is paradoxically the figure that threatens the whole edifice of patriarchy through the havoc she wrecks on the ideological foundations of the traditional family: i.e., "purity" of family lines—referred to as "race" in Sand's novels, and property transmission.

The negative impact of the mother figure on younger women is articulated in the first letters of the novel exchanged between Mme de Theursan's daughter Fernande and Clémence who make clear that the young women disapprove of the mother. Clémence calls her a "méchante femme/mean woman" (815), "la plus intéressée, la plus fausse, la plus adroite du monde/the most selfish, most hypocritical, and most skillful woman in the world" (824); Fernande admits that her mother is a greedy snob (she arranges a marriage between her daughter and the older Jacques because, although he is not noble, he has a big fortune): "My mother's eyes and ears were wide open to inhale the sound and view of this beautiful million" (816). Furthermore, Mme de Theursan is a liar: she fails to tell Fernande that Jacques is much older than she is (by 18 years) and falsely reports to Jacques that Fernande is happy about the age difference (817).

But Mme de Theursan is more than a calculating woman who only cares about money; as the reader will slowly discover, she embodies pre-revolutionary values according to which appearances matter above all else. She has brought up her daughter to be an obedient wife and to observe decorum at all cost (854). Fernande blames her own childishness and her ignorance on her upbringing (854). The mother's definition of virtue as the obligation to obey, of course, emphasizes the lack of power of women in marriage but, as will become clear, frees the woman from any moral obligations. In this pre-bourgeois notion of marriage where love is absent, fidelity has no place.

Mme de Theursan's patriarchal conception of marriage as a form of slavery is antithetical to Jacques' own notions of marriage as an equal partnership where the feelings of each spouse must be respected. His scorn of Mme de Theursan is clearly expressed when he tells his confidante Sylvia that one of the reasons why he is marrying Fernande is to "save her from a bad mother" (834). Later the reader will learn just how bad Jacques thinks Mme de Theursan is. When Sylvia presses him to admit that he is her brother, he admits that although he has no legal proof, he is certain of it. Jacques'narrative reveals the cultural anxiety created when a woman's sexual activity is not curbed; he explains that his dying father revealed that he had an affair with a woman who got pregnant and helped her abandon the baby at an orphanage because at the time she had two lovers and didn't know for sure whose child it was. Jacques does not reveal to Sylvia until much later that this woman was Mme de Theursan (thus that she was Sylvia's mother and that Sylvia is his wife's half-sister) but adds "Cela acheva de me faire haïr et mépriser cette femme/ this was the last touch that made me hate and despise this woman" (860).

This narrative of Jacques raises the issue of the consequense of a female sexual activity that is not confined to the marriage bed; i.e., that transgresses the patriarchal law that links woman's sexuality to the assurance that reproduction will serve to ensure the purity of lines of descent. The scandal of Mme de Theursan's behavior is not only that she is immoral (although her husband is not mentioned, she was obviously married, had two lovers at the same time, and abandoned her child), but that she has destroyed patrilinearity. A woman who makes it possible to doubt who the father is reveals how fragile the foundation of patriarchy is. Interestingly, while Jacques blames her for her corruption, he forgives his father (whom he simply calls "bon et faible/good and weak" and strangely enough doesn't discuss either whether Mme de Theursan was married when she had her affairs (which would make Jacques' father an adulterer as well) or whether his own mother was alive. Jacques' double standard (blaming the woman for multiple relations while exonerating his father who may have abandoned his own child) and his scorn about Theursan reveals that what is at stake is not morality, but keeping patrilinearity secure. His anxiety seems solely focused on the disruptive female character.

The unfaithfulness of a wife and mother like Mme de Theursan imply that any woman may be capable of such transgression (including Jacques' own mother) and imply that there is no guarantee that Jacques is his father's son. The only certainty is that Fernande and Sylvia are the daughters of Mme de Theursan and that Jacques is his mother's son. In other words, women's sexuality is a threat to patriarchal power since that power is based on the continuity of genealogical lines. Jacques' anxiety over the issue of genealogy resurfaces later when, near the end of the novel, he laments the loss of Fernande's love and the death of their twin babies:

> Je suis Jacques, l'amant oublié, l'époux outragé, le père sans espoir et sans postérité. Je pensais que posséder une femme par le mariage, c'était assurer autant que possible la durée de ce bonheur...Je m'étais créé une famille, une maison, une patrie...Dieu m'avait béni en me donnant des enfants/I am Jacques, the forgotten lover, the violated husband, the father without hope nor posterity. I thought that possessing a woman through marriage is to ensure as much as possible a long lasting happiness...I had made for myself a family, a house, a motherland...God had blessed me by giving me children (1009).

What haunts Jacques is the realization that creating a family may be the prerogative of women only. The existence of women like Mme de Theursan challenges the security of ancestral lines and the possibility that a man can own his "race." His reference to children as the gift of God is revealing: it erases the fact that it is his wife who has borne and given him the children. Through Jacques' anxiety, Sand explores the limits of gender difference, suggesting that the only intractable difference is precisely the difference that cannot be acknowledged by her hero: i.e., women's control of reproduction. Her tale of adultery and death of children is radically different from those authored by male nineteenth-century authors such as Balzac, or Flaubert. As Bill Overton has noted, in *Jacques* the loss of the children is not linked here to the sin of the mother (who has fallen in love with Octave), but to the deficient marriage (Overton 109). The children die, not as in the traditional novel because the mother is adulterous, but because the marriage is flawed (the husband is too old). When Octave learns that Fernande is pregnant he vows to stand by her and reassures her that the child will live and be strong because it is the fruit of their love. In other words, posterity is assured because the desire of woman is fulfilled, not because of patriarchal structures.

Sand thus uses Mme de Theursan both to represent the type of the "bad mother" and as a means through which she can test the claims of seductive heroic male figures who reject the hierarchical models of marriage but who, for all their good will, are unable to actually accept women as equal social, intellectual, and sexual partners. Sand's plot suggests that Jacques rejects a heavy handed patriarchal system where the wife's role is to obey because it is an ineffective way to control descent—the wife may obey while having affairs—not because Jacques is ready to experiment with a new set of relations where power is redistributed. In this regard, he is not unlike Indiana who rejects the tyranny of an imposed marriage but who then proceeds to enter a relation with Raymon that is equally patriarchal and oppressive.

As she did in *Indiana*, Sand creates a protagonist whose portrait is fraught with contradictions that suggest the difficulty of changing mentalities[20]: he is presented as a superior man who opposes mediocrity and patriarchal institutions but she constructs the plot in a way that reveals the limits of his feminism and his inability to think outside of the dominant patriarchal ideology. At the beginning of the novel, Sand makes Jacques articulate a position close to her own: a radical stand against the indissolubility of marriage. Jacques calls marriage a most barbaric institution (834) because it is based on coercion. However, he admits that people are not ready to adopt a better system ("les hommes sont trop grossiers et les femmes trop lâches pour demander une loi plus noble que la loi de fer qui les régit/men are too coarse and women too cowardly to request a law nobler than the one that reigns over them" (834). He rejects attempts at reform as utopian because "avant de changer la loi il faut changer l'homme/before changing the law one has to change man" (834).

Sand is using Jacques to demonstrate just how difficult it is to achieve what he advocates. Although his statement about the need to change men seems restricted to men less enlightened that him, Sand's plot reveals that he himself needs to change radically; if new relations between men and women are to be established, new divorce laws won't be enough. Early on, when he explains to Sylvia why he is marrying Fernande, the inconsistencies of his position become apparent.

Jacques' stated reasons for marrying Fernande are worth detailing because they bring to light Sand's critique of bourgeois marriage and of seemingly more progressive positions such as that of the Saint Simonians. As we have already seen, he wants to protect Fernande from the bad influence of her mother (and we know what kind of anxiety about women's sexuality his feelings against Fernande's mother involve); he also admits that it is the only way to have her (834). The precise meaning of having her includes satisfying his libido but also refers to one of marriage's hidden goals, i.e., making sure that the wife won't satisfy someone else's desire. It is remarkable that Jacques's lecture to Fernande about the hypocrisy of the marriage vows promise of everlasting love refers to *his* inability to love forever. He doesn't seem to consider much what will happen to her feelings. Sand's careful analysis of the function of "love" in the ideology of bourgeois marriage (i.e., hiding economic goals) is also accompanied by the suggestion that critics of bourgeois marriage such as the Saint Simonians who advocated freedom, had a point of view that somehow ended up serving masculine positions.[21]

Jacques' last justification for marrying Fernande seems to be a generous one: he wants to share his strength and independence with "un être faible, opprimé, pauvre et qui me devra tout/a weak, oppressed, poor person and who will owe me everything" (834). His recognition that Fernande is oppressed and his generosity are praiseworthy and have been praised[22], but the last phrase is telling: it establishes a power imbalance that is irreversible. As Sand will show in the rest of the novel, claims to mutual respect and equality between the sexes are impossible to sustain when one of the partners has all the power (intellectual, moral, financial, sexual, etc).

As in *Indiana*, one of the mechanisms of the victimization of women characters is the withholding of information, even when motives for doing so seem to stem from a desire to protect the women. Like Ralph, Jacques withholds information from Fernande and refuses to explain himself on numerous occasions, which leads her to distrust him. Sand insists on the importance of power imbalance and lack of communication to explain why the marriage of Jacques and Fernande is doomed from the start by providing a number of incidents that hammer her point home. For instance, before the characters' marriage, Sand describes a seemingly innocuous incident that contains the dynamic of Jacques and Fernande's relation. Fernande discreetly gives money to an old woman and accepts her effusive thanks with grace. Jacques is irritated by the compliments of the old woman, dismisses her curtly, and patronizes Fernande. She is willing to admit that she did wrong (although it is obvious that all she did was to be aware of the feelings of the poor), and asks him to explain his irritability, which he refuses to do (819). This pattern of silence caused by the assumption that his young wife is incapable of understanding his feelings is repeated throughout the novel and Sylvia even rebukes him for his unwillingness to explain himself (884). When he is sad or preoccupied, he won't tell Fernande why (876); when she asks him about a song he favors, he destroys the sheet of music rather than explaining to her the difference between a "romantic memory and regretting a forgotten love" (881). It is no wonder that Fernande is upset at not being treated as a companion. Jacques also fails to tell her when he is sick or when her own children are sick; although his justification is that he wants to spare her, his protective stance reveals again the power disparity between them. A last symbolic example of Jacques' unwillingness to communicate with his wife is his habit to speak Italian with Sylvia, a language that Fernande doesn't know.

In contrast with Jacques' silence toward his wife, he does share his feelings with his friend Sylvia but noticeably, he withholds from her until very late in the novel his knowledge about her parents, thus controlling as well his relation with her. As these examples of lack of intimacy indicate, and as Wingard Vareille has noted, Jacques and Fernande's relation is doomed long before the arrival of Octave as potential lover and Sand's later portrayal of Jacques as a noble, misunderstood man in love with his wife seems contradictory.

Although Jacques claims that he doesn't want to be loved like a master (891) and objects when his wife adopts an abject position (she kneels down for forgiveness), all he does nonetheless reflects his sense of control. He judges and assesses his wife at the very time he seems to express his admiration of her moral qualities ("je vous ai jugée sincère, juste et sainte/I judged you to be sincere, just and saintly"(818). His portrait of Fernande to Sylvia reveals Jacques'unconscious but significant patriarchal superiority: "J'aime une vierge, une enfant belle comme la vérité, vraie comme la beauté, simple, confiante, faible peut-être mais sincère et droite/I love a virgin, a child beautiful as truth, true like beauty, simple, trusting, weak perhaps but sincere and honest" (833). In other words, her appeal resides in that she is beautiful but totally controllable (she is inexperienced sexually, weak and poor). Jacques'attraction to Fernande is thus highly suspicious.

The repetition of terms indicating possession and control be it physical or psychological, demonstrate Sand's careful construction of Jacques's desire for control and his own lack of awareness. To make sure that the readers cannot escape the paradox of Jacques'claims (although many have), Sand closes Jacques'description with this comment "Le caractère de Fernande est ce qu'il est; je l'étudie, je le possède et je traiterai

avec lui en conséquence/Fernande's character is what it is; I am studying
it, I have control of it and I'll deal with it as it warrants" (834). Although
he laments his wife's childishness, descriptions such as these make clear
that it is her position as a child (i.e., her inferiority) that has attracted him.
Sand's paradoxical portrayal of Jacques thus demonstrates that "before
changing laws, you have to change the way human beings think." Jacques
has de facto changed the law and refused to behave like a traditional
patriarchal husband, but he is unable to choose a mate that would be his
equal and he cannot give up his desire for control.

Sand's undermining of the contradictions of Jacques' enlightened
position is buttressed by her carefully wrought description of the two
female characters who display a range of qualities and characteristics that
invalidate claims of innate femininity and that question gender differences.
Sand sets up these two characters in such a way that questions about the
role of culture in constructing gender become obvious. Fernande and
Sylvia probably have different fathers but share the same mother. While
their genealogy is similar[23], their upbringing and social circumstances have
differed. Sylvia was abandoned at birth and spent her childhood with a
family of harsh but loving Italian peasants before Jacques found her and
gave her a solid education, while her younger sister Fernande lived with
her aristocratic but impoverished mother before being sent to a convent, as
many girls of her class were, to learn social graces.

Both women are intelligent, sensitive, and insightful, but the
difference of circumstances in their upbringing leads one to become an
independent, strong individual while the other exhibits all the behaviors
traditionally associated with femininity. Like Indiana, Fernande is
ignorant, both intellectually and morally, as she herself realizes. As she
tells Jacques "Je suis une enfant, et l'on ne s'est guère donné la peine de
former mon esprit; mais j'ai le coeur fier, et ma simple raison a suffi pour
m'éclairer sur certaines choses/I am a child and little care has been given
to train my mind; but my heart is proud, and. reasoning ability has of itself
enlightened me on some things." (854). Fernande's admission of ignorance

is immediately followed by a statement about her inevitable position as an inferior "Ma mère m'a toujours dit qu'un mari était un maître, et que la vertu des femmes est d'obéir. Aussi j'étais bien résolue à ne pas me marier/My mother always told me that a husband was a master and that women's virtue was to obey. So I am quite determined not to marry" (854).

Fernande's two statements link her lack of education and her likely inferiority in marriage to her mother, who is here described as an agent of the patriarchal status quo. The lack of intellectual development and the gender inferiority of the daughters are showed here to be reinforced, if not created, by the aristocratic mother, as Fernande's situation (with a mother) and Sylvia's case (without one) makes clear. In both cases, the father is absent and in Fernande's case never mentioned. The task of acculturation thus rests entirely on the mother. Sand's representation of the mother as the means through which specific roles are transmitted is not a misogynist move but a suggestion that women have power, but a power used in the interest of patriarchy, and a demystification of the role of the mother in the private sphere as nurturing agent of natural qualities (i.e., femininity) as nineteenth-century Bourgeois ideology would have it. Here Sand shows that what is nurtured is far from being natural; it is in fact embedded in a context of power relations that seek to reproduce inequalities, be they gender, class, or generation inequalities.

Sand further shows that Fernande has interiorized those learned characteristics that place her in the "feminine" category. After she marries Jacques, she does not attempt to become more sophisticated: "Je ne désire pas non plus former et orner mon esprit; Jacques se plaît à ma simplicité/I don't want to train or enrich my mind. Jacques likes my simplicity" (870). Sand demonstrates how the ignorance characteristic of a young woman is "taught" by the mother to meet the husband's expectations (even a husband supposedly as sophisticated as Jacques), and is then claimed as a sign of seduction. Fernande claims her childishness in the same way Indiana had claimed her ignorance. She describes herself as a child that needs to be guided (889), and, although Jacques ultimately treats her like a child in good patriarchal fashion : "Il faut que je la traite en enfant le plus longtemps possible/I must treat her as a child as long as possible" (893), he is nonetheless aware that Fernande's weaknesses are the result of cultural context[24]. As he tells his friend Sylvia "J'ai horreur de ce tempérament de convention que la société *fait* aux femmes et qui est le même pour tous/I hate the conventional personality that society imposes on women and that is the same for all" (893). He contrasts Fernande's personality to Sylvia's: "On ne lui a pas *fait*, comme à toi, un corps et une âme de fer/She was not imposed, as for you, a body and a soul of iron" (892). Jacques here articulates Sand's position on the construction of gender personality. As a child, Sylvia was proud, sensitive, and intelligent (and so was Fernande). But a life of work in the fields with her adoptive parents made her strong like other peasant children—here Sand suggests that women's physical strength or weakness is a function of social class—and Jacques then provided her with a serious education. He recalls: "Il était temps que des occupations plus élevées and et des idées plus justes vinssent régler l'élan impétueux de cette jeune tête; l'éducation te devenait indispensable/It was time for higher occupations and juster ideas to rein in the impetuous movement of this young head; you absolutely needed to be educated" (865). The narrative of Sylvia's youth is radically different from that of Fernande and emphasizes the mechanisms through which Sylvia has become a superior being: "tout ton être, et jusqu'à ta vigueur physique, diffère des êtres qui sont autour de toi/your whole being, even your physical vigor, differs from the people around you" (865). Interestingly, Jacques speaks about "êtres," that is human beings who are not gendered as Sylvia is different from and stronger than not only other women but other men.

Comments such as these, which reveal Jacques to be as constructionist as Sand and unusually enlightened, of course, clash with Sand's presentation of the same character in other parts of the novel as a man who encourages the childishness of his wife and who wants to control the sexuality of women. Sand uses Jacques to express views that are her own but that can be better accepted by her readers when uttered by a male character that seems to embody an ideal of masculinity[25]. Jacques' assessment of Sylvia as a superior being unable to find her equal parallels his own situation but, as we shall see, Sand shows that his superiority stops short of questioning the nature of his own desires.

Sylvia's intellectual, physical and moral strength and Fernande's lack of these same qualities are presented as the result of specific circumstances, a position that Sand has repeatedly taken and which she reinforces through the mouths of several characters. Sylvia herself, when warning Jacques against marrying Fernande, asserts "elle est femme, elle a été élevée par une femme, elle sera lâche et menteuse/She is a woman, she has been brought up by a woman, she will be a coward and a liar" (840). Sylvia's comments again reassert that "women" are made (her statement that Fernande is a woman immediately followed and modified by the second statement that she was brought up by a woman transforms it into a causal statement "she is a woman because she has been brought up by a woman").

Sand's description of two women with differing intellectual and moral fibers but who began with similar potential is carefully conceived even at the level of details that seem inconsequential but that are a constant reminder of the role of culture in the construction of personality and of gender. A significant instance is voice. Fernande is described as having a very attractive voice (it is her voice that first seduces Jacques before he even sees her [819] as is Sylvia. However, Sylvia's voice has been trained and Fernande comments that her voice is so remarkable that she could be a successful professional singer—which she is not because she does not need to work for her living; she receives a pension from Jacques (906). Sand's interest in the voice is well-known and here she uses it as a metonymy for the female body to demonstrate that a "natural" physical characteristic is inseparable from its symbolic existence, whether it be its sexual or cultural significance. It also points to the paradox of Jacques' role in providing Sylvia with training, i.e., with a different gender identity. Thanks to the generosity of Jacques, she escapes the fate of most women (her voice is "trained") but also thanks to his generosity, her training is restricted to the realm of the private sphere. Sand hints at the complexity of what appears to be a positive aspect of the binary division of the sexes into protectors (men) and protected (women).

The last parallel that Sand draws between her two female characters involves sexuality and maternity, which she uses again to challenge notions of natural femininity. Although it has been stated that Sand, like other nineteenth-century writers, "reterritorialized" female sexuality into maternity, in a number of novels, and especially in *Jacques* Sand uses maternity as the sign and sometimes the consequence of sexual activity rather than as its cause. She uses pregnancy to remind the readers that women's sexual activities, especially when occurring outside marriage (i.e., when obviously separated from the goal of ensuring offspring) usually have dramatic social and physical consequences. Jacques himself lists the usual consequences of women's unfaithfulness and rejects them as barbarous.[26]

Whether sanctioned by marriage or not, Sand shows that the women's sexual engagement is part of their life. Both the conventional Fernande and the rebel Sylvia are or become sexually experienced during the course of the novel and link sexuality with emotions (what Jacques calls "love"). Sylvia has had affairs and been disappointed in her lovers, the last one being Octave. Fernande gets married in the course of the novel, becomes a mother, has an affair with Octave and becomes pregnant again. Sylvia breaks up with Octave when she realizes he doesn't fulfill her expectations: she cannot separate intellectual companionship from sexual intimacy, but as we shall see, she is willing to give up sex for companionship. Similarly Fernande, in the midst of her secret affair with Octave, recoils when she thinks Jacques has come to her bedroom to claim his husbandly privilege (957).

Sand also hints at the ideological construction of normally

unquestionable notions like sex drive. For in *Jacques* women are not the only ones to link the sexual and the emotional; men also do. Before meeting Fernande, Jacques is described as being a kind of seducer who has pursued a number of beautiful women whom he idealized until he discovered they were flawed (846). The major difference between Jacques and the women characters is the number of experiences he has had and the fact that there are no negative cultural consequences sanctioning a man's sexual and romantic experiences. [27]

Paradoxically though, Sand presents Jacques and Sylvia as divided over the role of heterosexual love. Near the end of the novel, Jacques' statement "Il n'y a pourtant qu'une chose dans la vie, c'est l'amour/There is however only one thing that counts in life, it's love" (1018) contrasts with Sylvia's own remark "Il doit y avoir autre chose dans la vie que l'amour/There must be something else in life beside love" (1022). Jacques has just refused Sylvia's offer to go far away, adopt children and bring them up according to their principles, rather than committing suicide as Jacques proposes to do in order to free his wife Fernande. Jacques' refusal reveals that it is not really "love" that he is unwilling to give up but the idea of a sexual partner. Life with Sylvia would mean giving up his sexual drive since he cannot separate companionship from sexual activity (which is what Sylvia proposes). Paradoxically, he hasn't had sex with his wife for one year because of her pregnancy and then because she was nursing (956), which puts into question the urgency of his male sexual needs. Through the contradiction between Jacques' practice (lack of sexual activity) and theory (the all-importance of "love" i.e., companionship and sex) Sand challenges notions of a "natural" male sexuality.

The narrative leading to the final scenes of the novel presents yet another contradiction in the hero's attitude toward the construction of gender, a contradiction that again suggests the difficulty of escaping cultural images of gender. It shows that Jacques' sophisticated understanding of gender construction is undermined by his attraction to women whose appeal resides in their sensual beauty rather than because they match his theoretical notions of gender construction. His physical portrait of Fernande reveals the gap between his radical views and his unexamined sexual desires. He describes her as very young, small, white, plump, blond, with a low forehead which, according to phrenology and to Jacques' description, would be a sign of mediocre intelligence (834). In the same breath, he mentions that she is "plutôt docile que saisissante/rather docile than striking" (834). In other words, he is attracted to Fernande's sensuality and naturalness, qualities that make her easy to dominate. By making Jacques the site of such powerful contradictions: he recognizes that femininity is culturally constructed but he experiences desires embedded in a patriarchal mode where the female object of desire is mostly a natural body, Sand shows how difficult the process of changing consciousness is (what Jacques earlier called the necessity of changing people before changing the laws). She anticipates the difficulties of conceiving modes of desire no longer structured by binary oppositions (male/female, dominant/dominated, culture/nature, etc), and the necessity to question notions that seem unassailable such as the nature of sexual drives or maternity.

In *Jacques* Sand represents maternity in a way that dispels notions of female instinct. She of course recognizes the biological facts of reproduction and lactation[28] as specifically female but she refuses to assign to them essentialist meanings. Instead she focuses on the care and love of children which is separated from biological function. Jacques is concerned that his wife lacks the maturity and wisdom to take care of their children[29] while Fernande objects to Jacques's interest in the children as unfitting a man's role (907). In both cases, they dismiss notions of instinct to focus on ability (in the case of Jacques's concern) or custom (in Fernande's case). However, the character who seems to know best how to be a mother is Sylvia, who hasn't had children of her own but whose intelligent caring seems to make her a strong mother. In a revealing incident in which Jacques and Fernande argue about whose turn it is to take the children, Sylvia interrupts the argument and takes them, claiming that the children are rightfully hers and later agrees with Fernande that she understands the bliss of motherhood (907). Sand presents a paradoxical situation where the mother is precisely the one who hasn't given birth and who stands outside the traditional nuclear family. She also valorizes the role of the father in making Jacques interested in the upbringing of his children regardless of cultural definitions of fatherhood. Finally, Sylvia's proposal to adopt children signals that motherhood is a cultural issue rather than simply a biological one. This reconfiguration of maternity moves away from biological difference (interpreted as inferiority in a patriarchal culture) to focus on other kinds of differences that are culturally mediated.

Sand's questioning of the mechanisms through which culture naturalizes binary differences finally includes the incest taboo. Sand's examination of the mechanisms through which culture naturalizes differences and oppresses women includes a consideration of the patriarchal requirement for exogamy. Her questioning of the foundation of patrilinearity and the anxiety surrounding women's sexuality leads her to question the uses to which the exogamy requirement (and the incest taboo that is universally used to ensure the separation of kinship) is put. However, instead of focusing on the father figure as narratives usually do, she concentrates on the effect on the daughter figures.[30] The primary instance of the incest taboo in *Jacques* is that evoked by Jacques to explain his lack of romantic interest in Sylvia, who may be his half-sister, but the novel also represents a number of relations that verge on the endogamous: Jacques' wife Fernande is the daughter of Jacques' father's lover, and the half-sister of his own presumed half-sister. Moreover, Fernande is young enough to be his daughter. These semi-endogamous ties do not deter him, however, from marrying her. At the end of the novel, as if Sand realized that Jacques's lack of interest in Sylvia was "unnatural" (after all she seems to be the equal partner he claims he would need), Jacques alludes to the impossibility of their being a man and a woman for each other (1025) because of his uncertainty about her father. However, Jacques's explanation comes too late to be convincing. The whole novel has demonstrated his attraction to beautiful, young women whom he can control. Thus here the male character uses the incest taboo to justify his lack of interest in a woman who would be his equal and threaten his position of power. Interestingly, while Jacques rejects Sylvia as a companion because of the possible confusion brother/lover, as we have seen, she is willing to brave the taboo. Jacques rejects the brother/lover model but has embraced the father/lover symbolic model, which suggests that what is forbidden is a heterosexual relation where male and female have equal power. Jacques repeatedly refers to his wife as his daughter or his child[31] and here does not seem to be bothered by symbolic incest. Jacques's submission to the patriarchal incest taboo is thus selective. On the one hand, it allows him to avoid relations that would jeopardize his position in the patriarchy; on the other, it enables him to justify marrying a daughter figure and keep his power. Unfortunately for him, his wife, no more than his friend Sylvia, does not want a father; she wants a companion.

Sand represented the failure of Jacques' position, i.e., his rejection of obviously oppressive patriarchal models joined to his inability to accept new models of relationships, by ending the novel with his suicide and with Sylvia's loneliness. This ending, which registers the difficulty of ending oppressive patriarchal practices and of reconfiguring gender relations, nonetheless signals possibilities for change: while in *Indiana*, the heroine's voice became subsumed to that of the male hero and her story becomes his story, in *Jacques* the hero realizes the limit of his attempts to change the world and his death allows his wife/daughter to live on with a man she loves, and to do so with Jacques' fortune. With Jacques' death, Sand avoids punishing the daughter figure, which would be a patriarchal gesture, but also demonstrates that the regime of the father is still too powerful to accommodate the new woman represented by Sylvia.

NOTES

1. See Sandy Petrey "George and Georgina: Realist Gender in *Indiana*. Pp. 133-47 in *Textuality and Sexuality: Reading Theories and Practices*. Eds. Judith Still and Michael Worton. Manchester: Manchester University Press, 1993.

2. She states "the story of Ralph recapitulates the writer's progress from initial uncertainty and hesitation to ultimate assurance and eloquence" (56).

3. Lukacher specifically argues that Raymon figures Sand herself "before the impasse of the double feminine identification " (77). Marilyn Lukacher, *Maternal Fictions*. Durham: Duke University Press, 1994.

4. This seems to be the view of the French editors of *Indiana*. See for instance the introduction of Pierre Salomon, ed. *Indiana*. Paris: Garnier, 1962; and Béatrice Didier, ed. *Indiana*. Paris: Gallimard (Folio): 1984.

5. See Nigel Harkness, "Writing under the Sign of Difference: The Conclusion of *Indiana*" *Forum for Modern Language Studies* 33.2 (1997): 115-128.

6. See Kathryn Crecelius, *Family Romances*. Bloomington: Indiana University Press, 1987. Like Harkness, Crecelius also believes that Sand posits a difference between men's and women's language (73).

7. Vareille focuses on the character of Delmare to show that, for Sand, the victims of mariage are men as well as women since they are also frozen in a social role over which they have no control See Kristina Wingard Vareille, *Socialité, sexualité et les impasses de l'histoire: l'évolution de la thématique sandienne d'Indiana (1832) à Mauprat (1837)*, 32-34.

8. I have showed elsewhere that Sand has constructed Indiana as a very strong character both morally and physically. See Françoise Massardier-Kenney, "*Indiana*:Lieux et personnages féminins" *Nineteenth-Century French Studies* (1990): 65-71. Vareille has also showed that while Indiana is presented as a "faible femme" who faints, cries, is emotional, she is also very strong morally: she attends to wounded men, she stands up to her husband, etc. As she will do later in *Jeanne*, Sand redefines traditional notions of physical and moral strength. It should be noted as well that the very characteristics that mark her as a "femme faible" (crying, fainting, etc) are also typical of the male characters: all three male characters cry at one point or another. Raymon faints when the body of Noun is discovered and Ralph almost swoons when he thinks Indiana died from a horse accident.

9. Although Indiana is clearly presented as the victim of patriarchal institutions and although the narrative is controlled by a male voice, it is her voice whether in direct discourse or through letters that is the most present. Even the prolix Raymon is not given more space in letters or actual speech than is Indiana.

10. While a number of critics have noted the link that Sand establishes between water and women, I maintain that they miss a number of occurences when water is associated with men as well. Noun does commit suicide in the river and, after wandering in Paris, Indiana, almost drowns in the Seine, but there are as many incidents linked to water that are associated by male characters: for instance, Ralph's early suicide thoughts, Raymon's near fall in the very river where Noun drowned, and of course, Ralph's later planned leap in the waterfalls of the Bernica. As I have showed in "*Indiana:* Lieux et personnages féminins," Ophelia is not a figure for women; it is the name of Indiana's dog and it is the dog that dies from drowning, not Indiana. When Indiana escapes her husband to sail back to France, the dog follows the boat and is killed by coarse sailors. It should not surprise us that Sand refrain from associating women with water, since it would be an essentialist gesture.

11. Sand's contradictory portrait of Ralph as a positive Romantic figure who opposes conservative social and political practices but whose own gender ideology is ultimately patriarchal will find a development in *Jacques* (1834), where she will explore the very possibility of the contradictions expressed by the Ralph figure.

12. Vareille Wingard notes the negativeness of sexuality for women: "for women, sexuality can only be a trap, a threat, an aggressive and destructive domination exerted by the male" (43), but she does not extend her remarks to romantic love in general which is also a domination exerted by the male in that it destroys the female's subjectivity.

13. Her evidence is mostly based on the fact that the word "virginal" is no longer used in the utopic episode (footnote 61, p. 63) and that Indiana dresses as a bride in the suicide scene.

14. Of course, Sand's decision to leave the couple childless is a further detail that marks the absence of sexuality from their relation.

15. In any case, chastity is by no means reserved for women: since Ralph's wife died, he has remained single and sexless.

16. See the Introduction for a detailed discussion of maternity as an irreducible gender difference.

17. For example Maryline Lukacher interprets Raymon's mother as a figure representing Sand's grandmother because her last words to Raymon are the same as those Sand's grandmother actually said to her on her death bed (77). Similarly Vareille Wingard, who is usually a very astute reader, fails to notice Sand's irony in depicting Madame de Ramière.

18. The theme of male narcissism and the role of mothers in fostering such narcissism will be developed and amplified in later novels, most notably in *Lucrezia Floriani* (1846).

19. See Bill Overton's *Novel of Adultery*, for a discussion of that tradition where women are punished for their sins.

20. The particular conditions in which Sand wrote *Jacques* may explain some of the inconsistencies—she wrote a chapter at a time and sent it from Venice to the publisher in Paris without a chance to revise the whole manuscript—but I would argue here that what we are witnessing is Sand's unfolding realization of the impossibility of the Romantic solution. While in *Indiana* it was still possible to present Ralph as a kind of solution to gender inequalities, by the time she wrote *Jacques* Sand's description of women's victimization and her analysis of patriarchy expressed her realization that the disenchanted Romantic hero was also part of the problem.

21. Sand could not have known it at the time, but the fate of a number of women who adopted Saint Simonian beliefs turned out to be rather grim. If the man with whom they lived left them, they led a life of poverty and two are known to have committed suicide.

22. See Dominique Laporte's article on Jacques where she presents him as the ideal hero.

23. Sand's downplay of the role of the father in determining genealogy was not mistaken; it anticipated by over a hundred years the results of current research in biology. See for instance Dorion Sagan. "Why Women Aren't Men." *New York Times* 21 June 1998, sec. 15:1+. After recalling that our culture is patrilineal, Sagan states "Biology tells a more matrilineal story: the tiny DNA-containing oxygen-using inclusions in all of our cells, called mitochondria, come solely from our mothers" (20). For a comprehensive biological study of sex, see Dorion Sagan, *The Origins of Sex: Four Billion Years of Genetic Recombination*

24. Here again, Jacques's unusual awareness of the cultural construction of gender seems hard to reconcile with his patronizing treatment of Fernande.

25. She was right in that: readers like Balzac obviously identified with Jacques whom they considered a superior man.

26. After he realizes his wife is in love with Octave and is pregnant, he muses "Il y a des hommes qui égorgent sans façon leur femme infidèle, à la manière des Orientaux, parce qu'ils la considèrent comme une propriété légale. D'autres se battent avec leur rival, le tuent ou l'éloignent, et vont solliciter les baisers de la femme qu'ils prétendent aimer, et qui se retire d'eux avec horreur ou se résigne avec désespoir. Ce sont là, en cas d'amour conjugal, les plus communes manières d'agir, et je dis que l'amour des pourceaux est moins vil et moins grossier que celui de ces hommes-là/ There are men who cut the throat of their unfaithful wife without further ado, as Orientals do, because they consider her as a legal property. Others fight with their rivals, kill them or send them far away, and go solicit the caresses of the woman they pretend to love; she recoils from them with horror or resign herself in despair. These are, in cases of conjugal love, the most common behaviors, and I say that the love of pigs is less vile and less coarse than the love of these men" (994). He closes his disquisition against common patriarchal ways of punishing adulterous women with a statement about the fact that you cannot command love and that no one is guilty for

feeling love. For Jacques, what degrades women is not a change of heart but lying (995). Here, obviously Sand is using Jacques to voice her own objections to the ways patriarchal culture usually treats women's sexuality. Within the historical context of the repressive Napoleonic code that targets women's sexual activities with particular severity, what is surprising is not the fact that Sand did not represent sexual women but that she dared articulate women's right to love and portray positive women characters who are also sexual creatures.

27. Fernande, who for all her naivete and ignorance, is rather insightful, is rather chilled at hearing the narrative of Jacques's former conquests. She wonders about a man "qui a déjà usé son coeur pour des êtres si méprisables/who has already used up his heart for such despicable creatures" (847). Although culture condones multiple adventures for men, she is aware of the inevitable emotional consequences.

28. The issue of Fernande's nursing is interesting in what it shows that Sand was well aware that maternity was used to focus women's sexual energies. She directly links Fernande's nursing of her children to her interrupted marital sexual activity. Octave becomes quite jealous when she stops nursing her twins and they are removed from her bedroom, which he interprets as a sign that Jacques will resume his sexual relation with her. Octave reproaches her "Vous êtes jeune, vous avez des sens; votre mari vous persécutait pour hâter ce sevrage...vous êtes redevenue femme, vous n'êtes plus mère/You are young, you have sexual needs; your husband was pressing you to hasten this weaning...you have become a woman again, you are no longer a mother" (956). Octave's speech reveals that he is aware that reproduction and lactation are cultural brakes to women's sexuality, which he acknowledges.

29. One could argue that she was mature enough to make the children, but we must recall Jacques's erasure of women's role in begetting offspring. See his comment on children as God's gifts.

30. For a history of narratives about the incest taboo, see Lynda E. Boose, "The Father's House and Daughter in It." Pp. 19-74 in *Daughters and Fathers*, Lynda E. Boose and Betty S. Flowers, eds. Baltimore: Johns Hopkins University Press, 1989. For a summary of the incest taboo from the point of view of the father, see David Willbern's "Filia Oedipi: Father and Daughter in Freudian Theory." Pp. 75-95 in *Daughters and Fathers*.

31. For instance, "tu seras ma fille chérie" (827), "mon enfant" (852), "c'est parce que tu es un enfant que je t'adore" (875), "Souviens-toi que je suis ton père, et que je te porterai dans mes bras" (958), "ma bonne fille chérie" (961), "Quand tu ne me permettras plus d'être ton amant, je deviendrai ton père" (1016).

CHAPTER II
FICTIONS OF UNDESIRE
FROM *LA DERNIERE ALDINI* TO *JEANNE*

Contemporary examinations of George Sand's novels have mentioned an inability or unwillingness to represent women's desire. Evelyne Ender has recently focused on Sand's representation of woman as a hysterical figure, that is as the woman who is "not supposed to know" (to parody the Lacanian expression) her own desire, while Roddey Reid has pointed out in *Families in Jeopardy* how nineteenth-century novelists (Sand included) promoted an ideology of domesticity and the "reterritorialization of women's sexuality onto reproduction" (35). However, it is remarkable that all these assessments usually rely on a very narrow sample of Sand's works [usually *Valentine* (in Ender's case), *Indiana* (see Leslie Rabine's essay), *Lélia* (Didier), or *La petite Fadette* (Reid)] and that they rely on patriarchal psychoanalytic explanations of the formation of woman's desire. However, as Kari Weil, among others, has demonstrated in her study of androgyny, both Freud's and Lacan's narratives about explanations of feminine sexuality are based on a single male model of sexuality.[1] Last these studies of Sand assume that there is a unity of women's desires; that one can speak of one Woman, one Desire. I would argue, on the contrary, that throughout her works Sand represents a range of desires (although most are heterosexual), of different kinds of women and of different intensity. Her representations of specific kinds of desire are anchored in socio-economic contexts that affect the expression and the satisfaction of these desires. Throughout her novels Sand bares the cultural mechanisms which restrict or even make impossible the emergence of desires in women characters who are disenfranchised simply because they are women. For instance, desire is a central focus of *La dernière Aldini* (1838), a novel that needs to be read in conjunction with the famous *Lélia* of 1833 and 1839, while lack of heterosexual desire is the theme of *Jeanne* (1844), a novel usually mentioned because of its pastoral setting. In these novels as in many others, Sand shows how the clashing of gender and class affects the experience, expression and realization of women's desires.

In December of 1837 as she was working on the revisions to *Lélia*, the novel that had made her infamous in 1833 for its depiction of Lélia's unsatisfied desires (both physical and metaphysical), George Sand was finishing her latest novel *La dernière Aldini*. During the few months she spent on *La dernière Aldini*, Sand did not mention writing her novel except for a note to her friends Frantz Lizt and Marie d'Agoult: "Dear *Fellows*, forgive my laziness or, to be more accurate, my illness and my work. I have had to work on both, for two months, a kind of rubbish/obscenity [cochonnerie] for Giumento [the public] that you will find in the *Revue des Deux Mondes* and which I advise you not to read unless you do it with your feet ..." (P. 290. *Correspondance* Vol 4. 26 Dec 37)[2]. Her preface to the novel itself minimized its importance and sought to make it look harmless. It was something she wrote at night in a hotel room and then, the next morning, forgot her writing in order to pursue her botanical interests and to chase butterflies with her son. However, Sand's use of the very strong word "cochonnerie" to refer to the novel in her correspondance suggests that more is at stake than she is willing to admit in the preface. "Cochonnerie" means rubbish (which is what Sand seems to mean in her letter), but also obscenity; it is instructive therefore to see in what way *La dernière Aldini*[3] constitutes an obscenity and how it is tied to *Lélia*, another example of obscenity of sorts since both novels focus on the desires of women.

Sand is accurate in calling *La dernière Aldini* a "cochonnerie" (i.e., rubbish) mostly because of its melodramatic plot, its excessive reliance on picturesque Venetian settings and dialect, and its improbable coincidences and careless ending. However, rubbish as it may be, it offers parallels with *Lélia* (after all, the male protagonist is a singer named Lélio), and it is a striking example of Sand's exploration of gender boundaries, of the intersection of class and sex, and a representation of the stakes of women's desires. This representation of a woman's desire and the threat it poses to the male character and to the social order is thus a cochonnerie of another sort, an obscenity, which the OED defines as something "offensive to decency and modesty," "modesty" being further defined as "woman's propriety of behavior, scrupulous chastity of thought, speech and conduct."[4]

The first two paragraphs of the novel are an introduction of Lélio, a famous opera singer by a third person narrator who seems to be a fellow musician and who admires Lélio for his moral qualities and his impeccable conduct with female admirers. Lélio himself begins the narrative by admitting that love has played a big role at two moments of his past and he launches into the story of his life. The son of a poor fisherman, he is sent to Venice to be an apprentice gondolier. There he hears a woman's voice accompanied by a harp; mesmerized by the music, he wants to see the harp and sneaks in the palace of the signora Aldini where he is chased by servants and ends up hiding in the attic for two days. When he is finally found, Mrs Aldini takes pity on him and hires him. Although proud, he accepts because of his fascination for the music.

Signora Aldini, the young widow of an aristocrat, grows fond of

Nello (as Lélio is known at that time) and arranges for him to take music lessons and to practice. She falls in love with him and proposes to marry him. Although Nello says he loves her, he refuses her offer, because he thinks she is too weak to brave public opinion (such a marriage between people of different classes would be sure to meet opposition), and he also refrains from taking advantage of her (i.e., he does not have an affair) although it is clear to him that she is quite ready. He leaves Venice, becomes a famous opera singer, supports the Carbonieri in Naples, and ten years later, performs at a theater where a young aristocratic woman in the audience disconcerts him with the intensity of her gaze. Lélio thinks he has been bewitched and falls gravely ill. He goes to the countryside to recoop with an old friend, the singer La Checchina. There, by chance again, Lélio meets the mysterious young woman. He is both drawn to her and frightened by her especially when she reveals that she fell in love with him the first time she saw him perform and that she is ready to marry him. His friend La Checchina advises him not to do so because of class differences. When he tells his young admirer that he would want the consent of her mother (which is an impossibility, he thinks), she reveals that her own mother had loved an inferior and would understand their predicament. Of course, Lélio's young female admirer turns out to be Alezia Aldini, the daughter of Bianca Aldini; Lélio is shocked and his "love" wavers. The young Alezia Aldini comes to his house in order to be compromised and force his scruples about the marriage. Count Stasi, a friend of Lélio and the owner of the house where he is staying discovers that Alézia, who had previously refused his hand, has come to the house to seek Lélio. Although Lélio makes bitter comments about Stasi's class prejudices, the latter helps him. Finally La Checca suggests to Lélio that he should let Stasi court Alezia since he loves her and they belong to the same social class. Having received a letter from Lélio urging her to come protect her daughter's reputation, Bianca Aldini comes at once and is very thankful for Lélio's help. Lélio leaves for Venice with Checca where they later hear that Stasi and Alezia are getting married. Checca takes things philosophically and ends the narrative with a hymn to freedom and Bohemia (254).

This complicated melodramatic plot should not hide the thematic core of the novel: the male character's association of desire with masculinity and his rejection of the desires of the three women characters. As she will increasingly do in her fiction, Sand relies on a first person male narrator, who is also the main character, to sap the very ideology he embodies. This technique allows her to represent the anxieties and the contradictions that are at the core of patriarchal power embodied by the male characters. Her representation of the coming to music of a male opera singer also challenges the nineteenth-century topos of the voice as something both feminine and inhuman (i.e. asexual, disembodied).[5]

As the plot summary just provided indicates, Lélio is invested with all kinds of moral authority before he even starts his narrative. However, before he can introduce the theme of his story (desire, with the implication that it is his desire) a brief description by the anonymous narrator clues the reader that the desires in question are not necessarily those of Lélio who is described as having a large dark eye full of fire that "attirait encore le regard des femmes/still drew women's attention" (131). Here the focus is on Lélio as an object of desire for women, rather than a desiring subject. The novel describes the feminization of men through singing and their rebellion against the desires they trigger through their own singing; music, or more precisely here singing, operates an inversion of gender position. Voice functions as the site where gender positions can shift, for being a male opera singer is to offer oneself as an object of spectacle, thus as an object of desire for a female audience. Lélio the singer represents the desire of the women who watch him. His position is ambiguous: although male, singing in public places him as an object of desire rather than as a desiring subject. The description of Lélio is immediately followed by Lélio's assertion of his masculinity and his association of desire with music. When he embarks on the story of his life, he focuses on the role love has played and he adds "vous comprendrez qu'il a pu m'en coûter un peu d'être, je ne dis pas un héros, mais un homme/ you must understand how difficult it was to be, I don't say a hero, but a man" (132).

However, as the story reveals, being a man has consisted mostly in shirking from the desires of women. This comment is followed by his vocalization of Beethoven's song *Desire* and comments about the superiority of German Romantic music over Italian music which is more sensual. These comments are couched in gendered terms where the male genius extends his powers " mais que notre génie étende ses ailes et ouvre ses bras pour épouser tous les génies contemporains par-dessus les cimes des Alpes/ let our genius spread its wings and arms to wed all the contemporary geniuses beyond the peaks of the Alps" (133). Lélio presents the ability to incorporate Romantic musical invocations as a further proof of masculinity. However his comments also imply a state of hybridity that may be a threat to the masculinity he is claiming.

His narrative suggests that his uncertainty about his masculinity is inextricably tied with his interest in music. He describes himself as very strong but "avec des contours un peu féminins, ayant la tête, les pieds et les mains remarquablement petits, le buste large et musculeux, le cou et les bras ronds, nerveux et blancs/ with slightly feminine shapes, with a remarkably small head, feet and hands, a large and muscular chest, round, nervous, and white neck and arms." (139). However, the assessment of his strength is in contradiction with his statement that his father found him so weak and puny that he sent him to Venice to work as a gondolier rather than teach him the fisherman's trade (134). Lélio's record of his humiliation at leaving home expresses his sense that he is leaving a world of men. He speaks about leaving "la maison *paternelle/* the paternal house, " the "périlleuse profession de *mes pères/* the dangerous professions of my ancestors" (134). Thus, from the beginning, Lélio expresses the tensions between the demands of an ideal masculinity (that of his father), and music.

His allusions to the fishermen's life as that of an unalloyed masculinity are accompanied by explanations about the role of music among the fishermen, a role that reveals again the association of music, hybridity, disorder, and desire. He describes fishermen singers called "Cupid" who not only mix all kinds of dialects but also improvise in the middle of reciting great poetry. The performance of these Cupids in which they mix dialects and registers, often triggers such a great excitement on the part of their drunken male audience that the singers have to flee. The attraction that Lélio feels for music is similarly accompanied by an awareness of the disorders it brings: gender and sexual disorders as we have seen, but also class disorders.

Lélio's familiarity with Bianca Aldini (a considerable breakthrough of social barriers) is caused by his interest in music. He steals into Bianca Aldini's palace to play her harp and, when pursued, he hides and faints from hunger. The breakdown of boundaries operated by music is here closely linked to women's power but with a masculine refusal to acknowledge that this power emanates from a woman's desires. Lélio explains that although Bianca is beautiful, he only pays attention to her voice, as if he knew that the power of her voice can be appropriated. Symbolically Lélio faints in the attic near the portrait of Saint Cecilia with a harp (138). Saint Cecilia, the patron saint of musicians is usually represented with an organ, not a harp. But here the harp is a reminder of Lélio's future patron Bianca Aldini; moreover, the fact that Saint Cecilia was a virgin martyr also announces Lélio's association of music with women whose sexuality will offer no threat to him. Sand's narration thematizes what Felicia Miller Frank has argued about the new role of the female voice in nineteenth century opera as that of Echo whose "role is to repeat Narcissus' words and thus figure his desire, her own elided out of representation" (63). Thus singing functions as a sort of narcissistic desire where the source of the music (women) is allowed to trigger Lélio's passion only to disappear. Although Lélio and his father are proud men, they accept Bianca Aldini's offer to employ him so that he can be near music, but Lélio makes it clear that no desire of woman is involved. He explains "Je ne sais quelle puissance magnétique la signora Aldini exerçait sur moi, c'était une véritable passion, mais une passion d'artiste toute platonique et toute philharmonique/I don't know what magnetic power Signora Aldini held over me; it was a true passion, but an artist's passion that was quite platonic and philharmonic" (139). When he explains his feelings for her "C'était de l'amour peut-être, mais de l'amour pur comme mon âge/Maybe it was love, but love as pure as my youth" (143) his explanation is not convincing: at the time Lélio was seventeen and cannot claim late adolescence as a period of inexistent sex drives. This initial lack of desire for her will be repeated throughout the novel with the other women in his life. In all cases, these women have desires of their own and express them, which may be what explains Lélio's lack of desire. He is attracted to women as embodiment of music, that is as an embodiment of his desire, but he cannot accept the autonomy of the women's desires.

Lélio's control of the narrative is undermined by the contradictions that run through it and through his presentation of Bianca Aldini. Although he often praises her beauty, her goodness and her meekness, he often repeats gossip that points to her moral weakness, her ignorance and her mediocre intelligence. He also criticizes her for spending equally on charity and on beautiful things, what he calls a "mix of feminine weakness and Christian virtue" (140). He interprets her taste for refined things as moral weakness whereas it could easily be considered as an expression of social and material power and knowledge, which would thus remind him of his inferior social position. His sense of his own superiority and of her inferiority because she is a woman enables him to minimize rumors and evidence that she was abused by her late husband. Lélio recalls that "elle se disait faible sur les jambes/ she said her legs were weak" (141), (implying that she did not really have weak legs), and that she always needed the help of two servants to go down the stairs. He further states that he never knew whether the rumor that she limped because her husband threw a piece of furniture at her is true, but he is ready to believe the servants' assessment of the husband as a cold, haughty man. However, later on, Bianca herself reveals to him that her husband married her for her money and despised her. Lélio's veiled hostility toward his patroness, which is expressed in his descriptions of Bianca, is linked to his resentment of her power over him as the source of music and her ability to give him access to music by allowing him to hear her sing, by having him take lessons, and by adjusting his workload so that he can go to the Fenice theater. It is also linked to the fact that as an aristocratic Venetian woman, Bianca Aldini has the power to express her need to love (as he euphemistically calls her having lovers (141)), to have desires and to express them. As a gondolier helper, Lélio has to witness her riding in the gondola with her lover[6] and he has to forego attending the opera and practicing his singing when she wants to go out. In other words her pleasure is an impediment to his own desire. Lélio makes an alliance with her lover at the time to gain permission to attend the opera (although separated by class, the men are unified because of their gender positions). The Signora Aldini readily agrees but Nello categorically refuses to sing for her. He finally sings in her presence one evening but he makes clear that he does so because of his own need to sing, not because of her desire to hear him (146). Although she doesn't react, he learns that she was stunned by his talent and he volunteers to sing again while she is in the gondola.

The pleasure she takes in his singing coincides with the defection of her lover and Nello's discovery that singing outside will make him lose his voice. Woman's pleasure is thus a danger for Nello: his voice, which he calls symbolically enough his "instrument," has been developed through the generosity of his patron, but her desire, which is expressed by her request that he sing for her, threatens his power. The complexity of the function of voice as the site where gender positions can shift is one of the core themes of the novel. For the male singer, singing privately confronts him with the desire of an individual woman while singing publically, as the readers were alerted at the beginning of the narrative, is to be placed in a traditionally female position as object of the gaze and of desire, with the twist that it is a woman's desire and gaze. Singing is thus directly linked to women's desires and constitutes a danger for a male whose own desire to sing is accompanied by uncertainties about his masculinity. Lélio's solution to his hybrid position, where his narcissistic desire clashes with the power of women is to deny them gratification.

As Nello's voice becomes stronger through lessons, Bianca Aldini's health fails: she becomes pale, weak, drives away her lover and refuses to remarry. It soon becomes apparent that she has fallen in love with Nello and that her love is connected to his passion for music, the common ground which was the occasion for the breakdown of social barriers (music is the justification for allowing him in her presence) and of gender barriers (her power through her own musical practice gives her the opportunity to become assertive).

However, Bianca Aldini, the rich and aristocratic woman is not a libertine, which would allow her to satisfy her sexual desires while remaining ensconsed in her class. Rather she wants, impossibly, as Sand demonstrates, within a patriarchal context, to fulfill her emotional and sexual needs, which can only be done by breaking down caste and gender boundaries. Sand shows that the male character cannot conceive of a woman's desires even if he could benefit socially by it. Neither can Bianca Aldini's in-laws who are ready to take away her adored daughter Alezia if Bianca is insane enough to marry outside her class; at least, that is what Lélio's fellow gondolier tells him. Sand shows here how the values of the upper classes and those of the lower classes do mesh when gender positions are challenged. As Nello himself admits, Bianca Aldini needs to love and to be loved as a whole person. Later she will tell Nello that men pursue her because of her wealth and position, which they want to acquire. Little does she know that Nello is no more interested in her personally than they are. For him, she represents music, she is the opportunity to appropriate the means to sing (she gives him the opportunity to take lessons and to attend opera at the Fenice theater); she never becomes the object of his desire.

It is striking that when he has to carry her down the stairs, he notes that he was overtaken with passion but this retroactive interpretation contradicts the rest of his description which focuses on the expression of her intense and active desires: "Cette taille souple et voluptueuse qui s'abandonnait à moi, cette tête charmante qui se penchait vers mon visage, ce bras d'albâtre qui entourait mon cou nu et brûlant, cette chevelure embaumée qui se mêlait à la mienne, c'en était trop pour un garçon de dix-sept ans/This supple and voluptuous waist that abandoned itself to me, this charming head that leaned over my face, this alabaster arm that clutched my naked and burning neck, this fragrant hair that mixed with mine, it was too much for a seventeen year old boy" (150). This scene, as narrated later by Lélio, suggests that Bianca Aldini is initiating the seduction; Nello's reaction seems to be generic (that of any seventeen year old year old boy) and his later descriptions of Bianca Aldini's attempts to be alone with him show him to be completely passive and to avoid any moves to satisfy her obvious yearning. In a highly charged scene in a gondola where they are both alone, he is at her feet and her eyes are closed but he doesn't move; he just complains that she is playing with him. Finally they get lost and in order to prevent him from crossing dangerous swamps, Bianca gets up and "trouvant la force de se tenir debout un instant, elle m'entoura de ses bras, et retomba en m'attirant presque sur son coeur/finding the strength to stand upright for one instant, she took me in her arms and fell back pulling me with her almost on her bosom" (155). Tellingly this scene doesn't end with Nello finally giving into her desire, but with her telling him she loves him and that she wants to marry him. He is stunned and wants to wait as he explains "Elle était enivrante, et j'étais un enfant. Néanmoins une sorte de répugnance instinctive m'avertissait de me méfier des séductions de l'amour et de la fortune/She was intoxicating and I was a child. However a sort of instinctive repulsion made me wary of the seductions of love and money " (159). In other words, when confronted with Bianca's desire and love, he reverts from the lusty seventeen year old he was a few pages earlier to that of a child (i.e., sexless) and he is horrified by what he calls les "séductions de l'amour/love's seductions." His repulsion has to do not so much with love as with the fact that Bianca, by expressing her desire, is taking a male role, and she is willing to mix social classes. He interprets her desire to marry him as a sign of weakness (she wants to hide behind the church) and he judges her severely "Je sentais qu'il m'eût été facile de surprendre les sens de cette femme faible de corps et d'esprit/I felt that I could have easily taken advantage of this woman who was physically and morally weak;"[7] (165) "je dois dire à la honte de la faiblesse féminine, que mes voeux eussent été comblés si j'avais eu moins de délicatesse et de désintéressement/ I must say to the shame of feminine weakness that my wishes would have been fulfilled if I had been less scrupulous and disinterested" (165). Translated, this means that Lélio finds Bianca obscene because she has physical and emotional desires and that she is willing to disrupt the social order to satisfy them. Ironically, it is Lélio, both lower class and an artist, a future Carbonieri who upholds the sexual and social order, although he self-servingly interprets his withholding as heroism.

The danger represented by the expression of feminine desire is restated even more forcefully in the second part of the narrative which repeats the same motif of the male character's rejection of a woman's desire when Nello the gondolier has become Lélio the opera singer and is disturbed during a performance by the insistent gaze of a young woman who, he will learn much later, is the daughter of Bianca Aldini. He is very disturbed by the spectator's "fixed and deep gaze" (172) and attempts to avoid it but is caught by its "mystérieux magnétisme" (173). A fellow actress tells him to beware of *La jettatura*, the spell witch-like women can throw and soon after Lélio is taken ill with a dangerous fever. This woman's gaze presented as so dangerous by Lélio turns out to be a look of love and desire, as we later hear that the woman was Alezia Aldini, who not only fell in love with him but did everything she could to marry him. Again, the very expression of feminine desire is interpreted by the male protagonist as a disruption of order: rational order as the allusions to magic suggest, sexual order (as the traditional dynamics of desire are reversed), social order (the desiring woman is willing to break social class barriers for her love), and psychological order (desire is expressed both at the physical and emotional level).

While the two women who express their desire are aristocratic women, that is their social and material position allows them to challenge gender rules and to initiate and direct the relation[8], the novel also presents another woman La Checchina, who acts out on her desires and whose attempts to marry because of love are also thwarted. Born in squalor, La Checchina is an actress and a singer whom Lélio discovered in the streets and who nurses him during his illness. She has had a number of lovers, all young, handsome and rich and is upset with her current lover Count Stasi who refuses to marry her. Lélio's description of La Checchina as a friend and a devoted sister (175) indicates that she is not his mistress, although the readers are led to believe that she may have been briefly at one point in the past. Lélio's lack of interest in La Checchina (who does belong to his social class) is explained by his repeated comments that her great beauty is "somewhat virile" (173, 231-32). Since he gives no details, the readers can easily assume that what makes her somewhat "virile" is her sexual assertiveness. Lélio's comments about his lack of sexual attraction for La Checchina (for example "Je compris vite que c'était une détestable amante et une excellente amie/I quickly understood that she was a terrible lover and an excellent friend" (196) need to be read with his assessment that she is morally and physically strong (197) and incapable of dissimulation ("null home ne L.I. semblait valoir la peine de se contraindre et de s'humilier à ses propres yeux par une dissimulation prolongée/she thought no man was worth the bother to restrain oneself and to humiliate herself in her own eyes through prolonged dissembling" (196). Lélio's admiration of La Checchina's independence and strength is paired with the implication that she is really not a woman. She is virile because she exhibits behavior that threatens his conception of normal women as weak, passive, and desireless, a conception that was widely found in nineteenth-century France.

It is therefore no surprise that the only instance of Lélio expressing his desire for a woman is expressed when he kisses Alezia's servant, an act, that is clearly an expression of his power as a male and a social superior.

Lélio steals a kiss from the servant in the context of his feeling overwhelmed by Alezia's assertiveness. He describes the servant as resembling Alezia (whose soeur de lait she is, a detail that emphasizes the similarity between the two), but she is "aussi naive, aussi douce dans son maintien que sa jeune maîtresse était résolue et rusée/as naive, sweet in her behavior as her young mistress was determined and cunning" (191). In other words, the servant is a true woman: modest and ignorant. The kissing scene also occurs immediately after Lélio's reflections on Bianca Aldini's domination over him (189). His recollection is of course at odds with the narrative that he himself has presented, but indicates that he perceives the very expression of a woman's desire as a threat to his position on the gender scale. Lélio blames Bianca Aldini for being a woman, i.e., for being emotionally, morally, and intellectually weak, but actually he does blame her for not conforming to cultural expectations of women as beings without desires. Because she has remarried, he blames her for being a slave to her social prejudices (225). He also blames her because she fell in love with "un home fort séduisant, mais assez mal famé/a very attractive man, but with a bad reputation" after Lélio left Venice. He also suspects that she would consent to her daughter's marriage to him, which he sees as a sign of weakness (224). All of these instances reveal, not so much Bianca Aldini's weakness, as the evidence that she has desires and that she attempts to satisfy them. Sand's rather coarse "ficelle" of the mother/daughter parallel, allows her to stress the point that Bianca Aldini's desires and her willingness to cross over class barriers extend to her daughter; in short, that they are not simply individual desires, but women's desires.

Sand's variations on the theme of women aristocrats or artists having, and acting out or attempting to act out their desires allows her to examine the different cultural mechanisms that deny that desire. It is no wonder that Sand both wanted Frantz Liszt and Marie d'Agoult to read and not to read *La dernière Aldini*. D'Agoult had precisely done what Bianca Aldini had failed to do: she broke with her social class to go live with a great artist who obviously had fewer uncertainties about his masculinity than Lélio. However, Sand may have realized that her choice of a narrative voice that embodies patriarchal constructions of masculinity and femininity may have appeared as a criticism of her friends and her focus on Bianca Aldini's sexual needs may have embarrassed them as well.

That is why perhaps at the same time as she minimized *La dernière Aldini*, Sand was bringing Liszt and d'Agoult's attention to her revision and expansion of *Lélia*[9]. There is obviously a great distance between *La dernière Aldini* and the *Lélia* of 1839. One was a traditional, popular, semi-realist novel while the other was an idealist reflection that moved away from the conventions of the novel and attempted to present in allegorical form Sand's philosophical and intellectual concerns. However, the two novels are linked by Sand's representation of women's desires, especially in light of the revisions she made to the first edition of *Lélia* which had appeared in 1833, revisions on which she worked while composing *La dernière Aldini*. It is well known that the critical reception to the *Lélia* of 1833 focused on the sexual impotence of Sand's heroine and her incapacity to experience pleasure. The critics also seized on Lélia's relations with her sister the courtesan Pulchérie and hints of Sapphism.

However, as Béatrice Didier has pointed out in her introduction to her edition of the 1839 version, Sand systematically corrected all the passages that could be interpreted as statements about the frigidity or homosexuality of her heroine. These corrections can be interpreted not as Sand's attempt to make her text more tame, but as a systematic removal of material the (male) critics could use to interpret the novel as registering the impotence of the main character (in a "blame the victim" sort of instinct), in order to focus on the cultural and social mechanisms that make the experience and expression of feminine desires improbable if not impossible. For instance, in the crucial scene where Pulchérie attempts to convince Lélia to throw herself in a whirl of pleasure with the men attending the party (Reboul:212; Didier: 194), Sand not only removed the material that could impute a lack in Lélia (sentences such as "I can't feel anything/je n'ai pas de sens;" Reboul: 208), but added narration in which Lélia explains her lack of desire for the male guests :

> "Vous aurez beau dire, Pulchérie, une femme n'est pas un instrument grossier que le premier rustre venu peut faire vibrer: c'est une lyre délicate qu'un souffle divin doit animer avant de L.I. demander l'hymne à l'amour. Il n'y a pas d'être bien organisé qui soit incapable réellement de connaître le plaisir; mais je crois qu'il y a beaucoup d'êtres mal organisés qui ne connaissent pas autre chose ....Ce sublime échange des plus nobles facultés ne peut pas, ne doit pas être réduit à une sensation animale/Whatever you may say, Pulchérie, a woman is not a coarse instrument that any boor can make vibrate: it is a delicate lyre that a divine breath must move before asking her the hymn of love. There is no well constituted being that would be really incapable to know pleasure; but I think that there are many poorly constituted beings who do not know anything else... This sublime exchange of the noblest faculties cannot, must not be reduced to an animal sensation" (194).

Sand begins by shifting the focus away from female frigidity toward the inadequacy of the male partner, the brutal boor who fails to make her "vibrate."

Although in his essay on intimate relations in nineteenth-century France, Alain Corbin notices that brevity of intercourse was the rule but that to consider the issue of simultaneous pleasure is anachronistic as "People [Here "people" means "men" I assume] did not pay much attention to their partners' pleasure" (592), George Sand did notice, specifically in her revised *Lélia*, the role of male behavior in the so-called frigidity of her heroine. Sand's reexamination of the nineteenth-century male fantasy of woman as angel (i.e., as a chaste creature with no sexual desires of her own) is accompanied by an attack on the concomitant fantasy of woman as "demon" to use Nina Auerbach's expression, of woman as a potentially insatiable and sex-crazed creature. For, Lélia may insist on every being's potential to know pleasure, but she also defines pleasure and love, not as sexual "instinct" (what she calls animal sensation) but as a complex construction of sexual, emotional and intellectual sensations. In other words, she refuses to separate the realm of the body from that of the cultural. Thus, Lélia's lack of pleasure stems, not from a female inability to experience pleasure (an inferiority located in the body) but from patriarchal constraints that equate pleasure with the satisfaction of male desires without recognizing the existence of a concomitant female desire and of a willingness to accommodate it. By switching from the term "woman" to that of "being" Sand denies that the potential for pleasure depends on one's sex; but by focusing on the conditions that make pleasure unlikely for women, she argues that the relation to pleasure depends on one's position in the gender divide. Lélia's insistence on the links between the sexual and emotional realms invalidates Pulchérie's position, that is a male fantasy of the happy courtesan who is fulfilled in the realm of the carnal.

Another instance of Sand's distance from traditional masculine fear and demonization of women can be found in her revision of Lélia's death. In the first version (1833), Lélia dies throttled at the hands of the crazy priest Magnus who is obsessed by her, whereas in the revised version of 1839, Lélia dies persecuted by the Church in an isolated and dilapidated abbey. The switch from a death caused by an individual male perversion to one caused by a patriarchal institution points to Sand's rejection of the representation of woman as the object of male desire and points to her representation of woman's autonomy as the object of a cultural prohibition. Béatrice Didier, in her essay on feminine bodies in *Lélia*, has noticed that Lélia is more "desired " than "desiring" (202) and that the novel thematizes Lélia's inability to experience jouissance ("l'impossibilité de jouir dont souffre Lélia" 202). However, the revised 1839 version reveals Sand's efforts to move from the "patriarcho-centric" notion of woman "suffering" from a lack; on the contrary it examines the cultural, religious, literary mechanisms through which jouissance and desire are denied to woman. As Béatrice Didier herself mentioned in her introduction to the *Lélia* of 1839, a study of the variants between the 1833 and the 1839 versions shows that Sand's later version criticizes a number of Romantic topoi, in particular those related to the glorification of Don Juan, the figure of male seduction, and to the importance of love for women. Lélia's decision to enter the convent is connected to her realization that women live in a situation of cultural dependence. Likewise, Sand's toning down of the exacerbated Romanticism of the 1833 version expresses her awareness that this literary movement represented a system of masculine values in which women could only be present as victims. [10] Lélia's abandonment of a literary (Romanticism) and cultural (the all importance of love for women) code in favor of religious aspirations based on a humanitarian faith in the future also translates another form of oppression. The established church persecutes Lélia, who in the 1839 version has become abbess of the Calmadules[11]. Religious structures, cannot, any more than literary or cultural ones, provide a space for Lélia's desires for autonomy. Thus, if Sand represents the female body as truncated, as a corpse, it is because she recognizes that literary representations of women's bodies are dependent on a point of view that is masculinist; she points out the artificiality of the female body thus constructed.

Whereas in *La dernière Aldini* women desires were mostly emotional and sexual desires, in *Lélia,* Sand represents desires that are intellectual, religious, as well as emotional and physical. While Lélia represents an idealized version of a superwoman, *La dernière Aldini* focuses on more ordinary women, but in both works, Sand examines the ways in which patriarchal constraints (expressed mostly through masculine self-centeredness and fear of women) contributed to silencing these desires. A few years later in *Jeanne* (1844), Sand would go back to the issue of the limits placed on the conceptualization of women's desires by focusing on the life of an illiterate and disenfranchised peasant woman. Sand's depiction of Jeanne's life provides a complement to her description of her previous heroines who were empowered socially (Bianca and Alezia Aldini) or intellectually (Lélia).

Although *Jeanne* is usually mentioned in the context of its position as Sand's first attempt to write a pastoral novel, it is fruitful to consider the novel as the continuation and culmination of Sand's fictions of female undesires. Sand published *Jeanne* in serial form. The impetus of the publication was, as usual, financial (she wanted to help her friend socialist Pierre Leroux set up a printing press in the nearby town of Boussac), and she obtained a very good advance to provide a serial for the pro-government *Le Constitutionnel.* The new owner was recruiting big names, Musset and Sue among others, to launch the paper. Out of these complex and confining circumstances, Sand managed to create one of the most powerful nineteenth-century meditations not only on the cultural, and socio-political transformations affecting post-napoleonic rural France, but also on the nature of patriarchal power and desires.

It is not surprising that *Jeanne* has been ignored in favor of more famous and reassuring novels like *La petite Fadette* and *François le Champi,* where power and desire are not so unrelentingly linked to patriarchal structures.[12] In *Jeanne* Sand shows that the heroine's lack of desire (of heterosexual desire) is linked to her intuitive awareness of the oppression exerted by the members of the patriarchy. Furthermore *Jeanne* is an instance of Sand's representation of the feminine as a concept that is constructed but that is made to appear natural in order to better disenfranchise those who fall within its definitions. Although Sylvie Richards has argued that the Sandian pastoral woman is "uninfluenced by the dominant patriarchal discourse" (367), I contend that an awareness of the power of patriarchal discourse is what motivates the construction of Jeanne as a virgin and that triggers her death. Sand's depiction of a variety of women (across different social classes and cultures) questions the very notion of a unified notion of woman by presenting different versions of women: for example, a number of her female characters endorse oppressive patriarchal values in order to use them to disenfranchise other women. Last, Sand also challenges stable gender boundaries by representing characters who unsettle strict oppositions of the masculine and the feminine.

The all encompassing and oppressive nature of nineteenth-century French patriarchal discourse is presented in the initial scene where Sand introduces her three male protagonists and her heroine Jeanne. Three young men (Boussac, an aristocrat with Romantic leanings, Marsillat, a liberal[13] bourgeois lawyer, and a wealthy tongue-tied Englishman Sir Arthur) are exploring a desolate countryside with dolmens when they come upon a beautiful young peasant girl asleep. They talk about her and before they go on their way, they each leave a coin in her hand. Years later, through a series of fortuitous circumstances, Boussac learns that the young girl was Jeanne, the daughter of the woman who nursed him and who has just died. To help protect Jeanne from her abusive aunt, Boussac has her employed by his mother as a servant. The illiterate Jeanne accepts reluctantly to leave the country for Boussac's castle. There she becomes the object of desire of Boussac who sees himself as a Romantic hero, of Marsillat who is a sexual predator and is used to seducing country girls, and of Sir Arthur who is smitten by Jeanne's beauty and extraordinary qualities and actually wants to marry her. Jeanne will have nothing to do with them for, among other things, she has made a vow of chastity and poverty. Her admirers and Boussac's sister, Marie, who is very fond of Jeanne, later find out that she made the vow at her mother's request, after finding gold and other coins in her hand when she awoke. She and her mother assumed that some ill-intentioned fairies ("fades") left the coins to do harm to Jeanne as peasants consider gold of ill omen. Although the superstitious Jeanne is told by Marie the "true" origin of the gold, she still insists on keeping her vow. Finally, lured by Marsillat to his retreat, Jeanne rejects his advances and, when she jumps off a window to avoid the shame of being found there by Boussac and Sir Arthur who have come to her rescue, she suffers a concussion and dies shortly thereafter in the

Boussac castle, mourned by Arthur and Marie Boussac.

The initial scene where the three male protagonists discover Jeanne asleep suggests the power of patriarchal ideology: Marcillat, although presented as politically enlightened, talks about Jeanne as if she were an animal. When he explains to Sir Arthur that the peasant girls in that particular region remain small until they are sixteen, he refers to her as "it" (ça) and adds that it is the same for foals and bulls (37). His attitude toward peasant women (considering them as animals to be taken advantage of or to be scared) makes the foreigner Arthur uncomfortable especially when Marcillat wants to shoot his rifle to wake her up. The "romantic" Boussac also wants to wake her up, but with the tip of his whip in a gesture that reveals complete confidence in his superiority. The disturbing physical violence their attempts suggest remains latent but is replaced by symbolic gestures that turn out to be even more powerful. The men decide to leave a gift of money in Jeanne's hand and to make a wish for her.

Although they act in striking parallel to the fairies of fairy tales, their wishes are more symbolic of the violence exerted upon the disenfranchised by patriarchal figures: Marcillat wishes her a strong man for a lover, Boussac a rich and generous protector, Sir Arthur an honest husband who will love and assist her (3). Their wishes demonstrate that a woman may only wish to submit to male authority, be it sexual (Marcillat), financial (Boussac), or emotional (Arthur). These wishes show that these men can only conceive of women's desires in terms of relations to men, and moreover that these relations express what the masculine figures want. Sand uses these seemingly benevolent wishes to express the narcissism of an all-powerful masculine patriarchal ideology that, while appearing to delineate a space for the feminine, actually erases it. Even Arthur, who is presented as an outsider whose place in the patriarchal order is problematic[14], reveals a conception of women as weak creatures who need protection.

The male characters' masculinist world view is in contrast with that of the narrator. Although the sex of the narrator is not identified, several things indicate that, male or female, it is a non-patriarchal voice that distances itself from the male characters it presents. Moreover, in the midst of the latent violence contained in the scene, the narrator provides a description of the sleeping girl that bypasses the male economy of desire adopted by the male characters. The description emphasizes the beauty of Jeanne, not as the beauty of a "woman" but as "human" beauty. The narrator compares Jeanne to ancient sculptures and figures of Greek art to emphasize her autonomy, her status as a subject rather than an object (of male desire).[15] The description ends with "La véritable beauté est toujours chaste et inspire un respect involontaire/True beauty is always chaste and inspires an involuntary respect" (38). In other words, true beauty puts a halt to patriarchal urges to reduce a subject to a body to be "owned" or assimilated. The narrator's effort to describe Jeanne from a non-patriarchal point-of-view and to valorize her humanness, as opposed to her belonging to a disenfranchised gender and class is in contrast with the narrator's later comments about the sociology of the region where women, who are often beautiful, often end up working as servants and, if pretty enough, providers of sexual services[16] in city households (44).

The gift of coins, although harmless on the surface, is also an expression of patriarchal values and violence. The men assume that a gift of money to a poor peasant girl will be welcome but of course the opposite is true. The obvious reason is peasants' superstition and in their beliefs in fades, the mysterious female creatures who can do good or bad. As Jeanne explains later "L'or, on croit chez nous que ça porte malheur/ among us, we think gold brings bad luck" (85). However, she follows with a perfectly rational explanation of her superstition: "Toutes les fois qu'un bourgeois en a montré à une fille, elle a quasiment perdu l'esprit, et elle s'est *rendu à lui*/Everytime a bourgeois showed some [money] to a girl, she almost lost her mind and gave in" (197). Thus when Jeanne finds the gold she thinks bad spirits acted as if they thought they had bought her. Jeanne interprets the gift as a possessive gesture; she is right of course since the gift was made by men who believe that as a woman and as a peasant, she is inferior to them. Her mother's and her own reaction (to get rid of the gold and to make a vow of chastity and poverty) indicate that they understand all too well the mechanisms of oppression. As a poor woman, Jeanne's relations with men are necessarily relations of inequality and the only thing she can do to escape oppressive patriarchal structures is to disengage herself from patterns of circulation, be they financial, sexual or familial. [17] Jeanne's vow of chastity is not presented as a hardship but as a choice, as a statement about the impossibility of heterosexual relations within a patriarchal context; an impossibility determined not only by her being a woman but also marked by her belonging to an oppressed class.

Her lack of desire (for heterosexual relations and for money) is expressed in her language, and more precisely in the kinds of songs she sings[18]. Whereas her village friend Claudie (who was seduced by Marcillat and who also comes to work in the Boussac castle) sings traditional songs with sexual innuendos, Jeanne sings songs about oppression (like the song of the peasant mourning times of misery during feudal times [323]). We are told that Jeanne's mother has explained to her that she should not sing songs she doesn't understand because it attracts bad spirits who make the singers crazy (like Claudie). The mother correctly sees that bawdy songs cannot be understood by the young shepherdesses because these songs express the desires of men and victimize girls. Thus the domain of the sexual is avoided, not because of any prudery or incapacity to feel, but because for peasant women, sexual encounter means male pleasure and female victimization.

Jeanne's lack of heterosexual desire thus expresses an attempt to escape oppressive patriarchal structures. However, it is more than a negative kind of withdrawal since Jeanne had, when she was growing up, at her disposal another non-patriarchal structure which emphasizes the bonds between mother and daughter and a system of beliefs based on traditions of Druidic times that empower women. Jeanne's mother's death is catastrophic for Jeanne because her mother was her protector and her death symbolically coincides with the burning of her house and Jeanne's departure from her familiar and familial world. Jeanne's mother, Tula is presented as an exemple of the good witch. She is said to have "la connaissance" (the knowledge) and she protects and initiates Jeanne in her beliefs. As we have already seen, Tula warned Jeanne of the dangers of gold and love songs. More positively, she has loved Jeanne, allowed her to be herself, and protected her. Jeanne recalls her mother's worries when she was out in the dark rain (77); her good humour (she did not yell, she laughed, told stories, sung songs (111); when Jeanne dreams, she associates her mother with the good fades who watch over her to keep the wolves away from her herd (915). In brief she recalls her mother's effortless nurturing. The narrator also intimates that only Jeanne's mother knew her great value as a human being (74); a comment in stark contrast with the narrator's following remark that for Marsillat Jeanne was beautiful but dumb as a swan (75).

Jeanne's beliefs are inherited from her mother (here the realm of the imaginary and the symbolic are intertwined), and although the priest and others question these beliefs, Jeanne stands firm "ma mère y croyait, et je crois ce qu'elle m'a dit/my mother believed in them and I believe what she told me" (84). Her stubbornness, however, is not presented as a sign of simplemindedness but as a mark of wisdom. When the well-meaning priest presses her to reconsider her vow so that she could marry Sir Arthur she resists and tells him that "Ca me faisait plaisir de lui obéir, et de plaire aussi à la sainte Vierge, et de ressembler à la Grande Pastoure/ It gave me pleasure to obey her, the Virgin Mary and to look like Joan of Arc, the great shepherdess." Jeanne places herself under the authority of a feminine tradition and rejects the priest's appeal to the Pope. She tells him that she cannot break her vow because she did it in the *"freedom of my pure will"* [emphasis mine] (278). Earlier when Sir Arthur had asked her who she would like to marry as he is rich enough to fulfill her wishes and endow her well, her answer is clear "Je ne suis amoureuse de personne, et personne ne me fait envie pour le mariage/I am not in love with anybody and I don't feel like having anyone in marriage" (177)[personne ne me fait envie pour le mariage]. Jeanne's use of words like "envie" (desire) and pleasure indicate that she knows what desire is, but that for her, desire is not linked to a relation with a man. She interprets as freedom her decision to live without heterosexual relations, as she knows they will inevitably destroy her free will.

Jeanne's beliefs, clearly transmitted by her mother[19], involve a return to pre-Christian times and are based on a tradition of women's power. As Jeanne explains "Elle savait seulement, par sa mère....des femmes saintes, qui, vivant dans le célibat, avaient protégé le pays et initié le peuple aux choses divines/She only knew through her mother....saintly women, who living in celibacy, had protected the country and initiated the people to divine things" (233). The narrator adds that Jeanne confused these priestesses in her imagination with the fades; and legitimates these beliefs by commenting that in places covered with druidic stones and caves devoted to druidesses, people use the terms "fades" or "femmes" (women) without distinction (233). These traditions link the power and knowledge of female priests with lack of heterosexual relations. The narrator thus uncovers a strand of feminine autonomy that links druidesses, fades, Joan of Arc and Jeanne, and that bypasses male desire.

Sand, however, does not create a utopian gynocentric world where women are good and men are all patriarchal figures. On the contrary, she shows that both in the ancient traditions of the Gauls and the depiction of her characters, many women have espoused patriarchal values. She thus distinguishes between negative women and positive ones, the latter being less common than the others. First, when the priest explains the topography of the land to Boussac, two traditions emerge: a healing one, that of Ep-Nell, an unofficial cult, where the druidesses lived harmoniously without a leader, a tradition leading to women who have "the knowledge," and cure the sick (women like Tula and Jeanne (188); the second tradition is that of Jo-mathr, representing the official cult, a site where human sacrifices were held, and leading to a negative form of witchcraft involving thievery, bad advice to girls, and poisoning of neighbors' sheep. This tradition is represented by Jeanne's aunt La Grande Gothe and her thieving accomplice Raguet. These two strands merge in the belief in the fades who, as Jeanne explains, are "des femmes qu'on ne voit pas, mais qui font du bien ou du mal/women you can't see, but who do good or evil" (84).

Although presenting a positive version of matriarchy (with the character of Tula), Sand presents it as a minority position. The other adult female characters are bad mothers: there is La Grande Gothe who not only steals, but abuses Jeanne and helps bourgeois men to seduce girls like Claudie. Gothe, we are told, is friendly with rich and dissolute bourgeois men and "handles" their secret affairs. She even takes money from Marsillat to facilitate his access to her own niece. There is also Madame Boussac who is presented as incapable of protecting her children and who caused Jeanne's mother to be fired without reason. Then there is her friend Madame Charmois who is attempting to ensnare any rich man to marry her mediocre daughter and who is willing to temporarily throw Boussac into Jeanne's bed before having him marry her daughter.

These women are the bad mothers who have adopted patriarchal values and are willing to sacrifice daughter figures to their greed or lust for power. Their association with patriarchal oppressive and hierarchical structures indicates Sand's refusal to equate gender differences with biological and even cultural differences. Sand is suggesting that notions of the feminine and the masculine have everything to do with one's position with regard to patriarchal power. Grande Gothe and Mme Charmois for instance who so clearly belong in the patriarchy, although they are women, are associated with the masculine and participate in the oppression of women by facilitating their exchange and their treatment as inferior objects. The narrator casually mentions that Grande Gothe has a masculine walk and speech (118), and that Mme Charmois has the mind of a "chief of police," a symbolic position in a patriarchal order.

Sand's distinction between positive and oppressive women is also symbolically made through her use of names. She opposes first names to patronymic names which make obvious the connection between these women and male patriarchal power. The bad mothers are all identified by a patronymic name: La Charmois, Mme Boussac, La Grande Gothe, whereas the positive women figures are often only known through their first Name: Tula, Jeanne, and even Claudie, as if the first name signaled a space outside of masculine power structures. Sand's careful use of first names reminds us of the linguistic and cultural mechanisms through which gender is constructed. In order to show that gender is constituted by the space which specific bodies are allowed to occupy, she plays with the opposition of patronymic names and first names when she introduces characters that are ambiguously situated on the gender divide. For instance, Marie Boussac who is an aristocrat and closely linked to the Romantic values of her brother, is also the only character who appreciates Jeanne and who links her to the tradition of feminine heroism associated with Joan of Arc. Another character who straddles the masculine and the feminine is the rich Englishman who wants to marry Jeanne. The narrator mentions his last name (Harley), but most often he is called "Sir Arthur," "Arthur" or "l'anglais" in a gesture that signals his ambiguous association with masculine values.[20]

However, playing with patronymic codes is not the only way Sand explores the mechanisms of gender construction. She also reconsiders the association of the feminine with weakness and of the masculine with strength. The women associated with non-patriarchal, feminine values, like Jeanne and Tula, are very strong physically and morally, but the narration makes clear that they are not masculine. Jeanne's strength in particular is emphasized, first when she enters her burning house to rescue the body of her mother (103); then when she nurses Boussac back to health (he recalls that she carried him in her arms like a child [193]). She can go without sleep for days. More significantly Jeanne is not afraid of a physical struggle with Marcillat because, as she says, she had enough physical strength (190) to ward him off. Actually after the incident where he locks her in his isolated room to seduce her, she forgives him in those terms "Il n'est pas méchant....Je suis plus forte qu'il ne croit, et il ne m'aurait jamais embrassée/He is not mean.... I am stronger than he thinks and he could never have kissed me" (270). Jeanne is thus presented as physically and morally strong and aware of her strength but the narrator is careful not to masculinize her: "la vigueur de ses formes n'avait rien de masculin/the vigor of her body, was in no way masculine" (141)[21]. This alliance of the feminine and strength is contrasted with the other peasant servant Claudie, who while wearing her aristocratic mistress's clothes, looks like a "d'un méchant petit garçon mal déguisé en femme/mean little boy disguised as a woman" (141). What makes Claudie "like a boy" is precisely her having succumbed to the charms of Marcillat's money and discourse, and thus to have adopted masculine values. Sand is here redefining a type of physical strength that is not "masculine" in that it is not associated with predatory, aggressive behavior, but with the ability to defend oneself[22] and to nurture others. Sand takes a gender stereotype about the physical weakness of women but rather than make her women characters like men, she lays bare the constructed association of force with aggression and the erasure of force as nurturing. Sand is arguing that the association of the feminine with weakness is a way to naturalize a conception of force that validates an oppressive patriarchal system and that devalues forms of strength that would challenge such patriarchal inequalities.[23]

Sand's description of Jeanne's strength is crucial for a proper understanding of her leap from a window and of her subsequent death. The few critics who have mentioned *Jeanne* usually mention Jeanne's leap as an attempt to escape being raped by Marcillat[24]. However, the narrator's repeated remarks about Jeanne's physical power suggest that such is not the case.[25] Jeanne does not become a victim because of physical inferiority but because of her lack of control over the patriarchal discourse that controls her world. After her fall and during her last moments she explains to Sir Arthur why she jumped and in particular that she did it because of the shame of being found by them [Arthur and Boussac arrived at Marcillat's door to rescue her and started pounding on the door], and of not being able to defend herself against "what he would tell you against me" (270).

Jeanne's fear of Marcillat's control of discourse and his ability to use it to discredit her is well founded. Sand has made repeated comments that Marcillat does not resort to force for his conquests but to bribery and sweet talk.[26] His lawyerly eloquence has had no effect on Jeanne but she assumes that it will convince Arthur and Boussac of her victimization. She sees an ideological alliance of the male figures through what she perceives as their common control of discourse. Her assumption that they will believe Marcillat's version rather than her own expresses her awareness of her own linguistic disenfranchisement. Of course, she fails to take into consideration that Sir Arthur's status as a member of the patriarchy is ambiguous. Her association of Arthur with masculine structures is based on her awareness of his social position, his financial power and his position as a well-meaning protector who occupies a superior position in the social hierarchy. Because of her own exclusion from patriarchal discourse, Jeanne cannot realize that Arthur is also an outsider. However, the narrator makes explicit similarities between Arthur and Jeanne in terms of their distance from patriarchal discourse. Arthur has a sort of "une sorte d'enthousiasme permanent pour les idées sublimes, qui n'avait pas trouvé d'expression, et qui paraissait un état calme parce que c'était un état chronique/permanent enthusiasm for sublime ideas that had not found expression and which seems a state of calm because it was a chronic state" (175) In this sense he had mysterious affinities with Jeanne's character. The narrator adds details to Arthur's description that emphasize his inability to control discourse. He was laconic, lacked verbal brilliance, was confusing and became incomprehensible in French (176). Sir Arthur is thus situated, like Jeanne, outside language and his exclusion is intensified by his foreignness, which becomes a sign of his being an outsider in terms of gender as well. However, his position in terms of class situates him within the patriarchy and balances his linguistic disenfranchisement.

Jeanne's own relation to language is explicitly and exclusively one of "foreignness." After comparing Jeanne to a Gaul version of the goddess

Isis, a defunct tradition of feminine values, the narrator adds "ne trouvant pas de sens au langage des hommes/she did not find any sense in the *language of men*" (169). Her linguistic disenfranchisement, uncompensated by power in terms of class as is Sir Arthur's case is thus ultimately the reason of her death.

In *Jeanne* Sand has challenged conventional distinctions between the realm of the feminine and the masculine and investigated notions of intrinsic physical, intellectual, and moral differences between the sexes. Her demonstration that gender categories serve to naturalize the oppression of a specific group of human beings, and thus overlap with class divisions explains the "undesire" of her woman protagonist Jeanne. As a poor, illiterate, peasant woman without access to any subject position or to the dominant discourse, Jeanne cannot have any desire. Although her male counterpart Sir Arthur is situated as an outsider, his position of power and control in terms of gender and class compensate for his tenuous relation with patriarchal discourse, which explains why he has and expresses desires. Remarkably though, his desire to marry Jeanne is a desire for the same, for one who, like him, unsettles patriarchal constructions and whose social disenfranchisement he can erase because of his own wealth. His desire for Jeanne is a desire to cut through the cultural mechanisms that oppress human beings but it is a utopian desire. Revealingly, on her death bed, Jeanne orchestrates Sir Arthur's union with her admirer Marie Boussac who is his social peer. Jeanne knows what social alliances are possible in the realm of patriarchy.

The ending of *Jeanne* reveals Sand's pessimistic view of gender and class oppression: its mechanisms are so strong that the individuals caught on the wrong side of the gender or class divide are doomed. However, her representation of Jeanne as a woman with no desire represents an effort to claim an unalienable self-sufficiency for the feminine, and a questioning of the notion of "desire" as an oppressive construction for feminine figures whose existence as subjects is denied. From Bianca Aldini through Lélia to Jeanne, Sand shows how problematic our modern Freudian bourgeois notions of desire are when they fail to take into consideration the restrictions placed upon the "feminine," let alone elusive notions of "feminine desire."

NOTES

1. For a discussion and assessment of Freud's essay on Femininity, see Kari Weil's *Androgyny and the Denial of Difference* (Charlottesville: University of Virginia Press, 1992) where she describes Freud's faith in a unitary origin of desire before sexual difference and where she uses Luce Irigaray's deconstruction of Freud's "dream of symmetry" and its effacement of sexual difference within a "self-referential system of male subjectivity" (11).

2. Sand was to repeat her injunction to Liszt and Marie d'Agoult not to read her novel a second time a few days later but one cannot help wondering why she specifies where she has published it. Perhaps, it is precisely that she does want them to read it even though she is distancing herself from the work.

3. *La dernière Aldini* was published in December 1837 and January 1838 in serial form in the *Revue des Deux Mondes*. It was published in book form and Sand's publisher Buloz noted that it sold well (cf note by Georges Lubin, *Correspondance* IV, p. 641). It was also translated into English in 1847 by a Miss M. Hays. London: Churton, 1847. This edition comprised six volumes and *La dernière Aldini* was the first title translated, another indication of its popularity. However, there are no scholarly studies of *La dernière Aldini* although David Powell mentions it in a few sentences as one of the Venetian tales in his survey of Sand's fiction. See David Powell A., *George Sand*. Boston: Twayne Publishers, 1990.

4. In this regard, *La dernière Aldini* provides a useful counterexample to Reid's generalization, based on his study of *La petite Fadette* in his *Families in Jeopardy: Regulating the Social Body in France 1750-1910* (Stanford: Stanford University Press, 1993) that Sand does not subvert the notion of the domestic family.

5. For a discussion of singing as something associated with the feminine and the angelic, as a sexless object of aesthetic pleasure by a male audience, see Felicia Miller Frank, *The Mechanical Song, Women, Voice, and the Artificial in Nineteenth-Century French Narrative* (Stanford: Stanford University Press, 1995). Miller Frank comments are directed at *Consuelo* but it would be interesting to include *La dernière Aldini* to show how Sand opposes this de-humanization of the feminine through voice.

6. He blames her for showing affection to her lover in the presence of himself and the older gondolier at her service. By doing so, he is claiming an individuality and equality for himself unusual for the times. Throughout the first half of the nineteenth-century servants were admitted in the privacy of their masters precisely because they were not considered sexual beings. The fact that Bianca Aldini does come to consider Lélio as not only a sexual being, but also a human being bears witness to her disengagement from the ideology of her class. For a discussion of the status of servants in nineteenth-century France, see Michelle Perrot's essay in *History of Private Life*, p. 234.

7. The French "les sens" has no equivalent in English. It means something like sexual instinct, physical sensations linked to the sexual. Interestingly enough, the Lélia of the 1839 version which Sand was revising while she was writing *La dernière Aldini* also alludes to "les sens" about women; in her case, claiming that she has no "sens," that is that she can't experience sexual pleasure. Here, the scandal for Nello seems that Bianca has "sens" that are easily awakened.

8. While it is difficult to make sweeping generalizations about sexual mores in nineteenth-century France, and thus to provide a context in which to read the originality of the women characters Sand presents here, one can point out to the restraining effects of the Napoleonic code which treated adultery, when committed by women, as a crime, and which stripped them of financial autonomy. Moreover, according to Michelle Perrot's description in "The Family Triumphant" (*A History of Private Life*: 99-129),the bourgeois nuclear family became the norm, which is to say that women like the Aldinis (aristocrats), or La Checchina (an artist) would be outsiders and perhaps less constricted by bourgeois morality. However, Sand demonstrates that these women cannot escape patriarchal law, which prevails even in artistic or anti-conservative circles.

9. Sand had been working on revising *Lélia* since 1836 after she signed an agreement with her editor Buloz in December 1835 in which she agreed to present revised versions of the works Buloz already had under copyright. She worked on and off on the revisions of *Lélia* for several years, but turned her full attention to it after she finished *La dernière Aldini*. For detailed accounts of *Lélia*'s genesis and reception, see Pierre Reboul's edition of the 1833 version (Paris: Garnier, 1960) and Béatrice Didier's edition of the 1839 version (Grenoble: Glénat, 1987).

10. For a convincing reading of Romanticism and *mal du siècle* as a masculine mode, see Margaret Waller's study *The Male Malady: Fictions of Impotence in the French Romantic Novel* (New Brunswick: Rutgers University Press, 1993). See in particular chapter 6 "Toward a Feminist Mal du Siècle: Sand's *Lélia*" where Waller analyzes Lélia's impotence

in the 1833 version.

11. The episode of the Calmadules and of Lélia's doomed utopian evangelism are linked to Sand's awareness of the difficulties of the real priest Félicité de Lamennais whose efforts to reform the Catholic church finally led to his excommunication. They also seem to express Sand's awareness of the masculinist limitations of Lamennais's own religious reforms. Although, in 1837, Sand had agreed to publish "Lettres à Marcie," a series of letters about women's role, for Lamennais's publication *Le monde*, a careful analysis of the narrative structure of the (symbolically) unfinished series shows Sand's uneasiness about the ideology she had agreed to promote, and her chafing under Lamennais's editorial censorship. Lélia's failed efforts in the religious realm may well be linked to Sand's understanding that religious rebels (i.e., Lamennais), like literary rebels (i.e., the Romantics), failed to question gender power structures.

12. Although *Jeanne* still needs to be "discovered" we now have a very useful scholarly edition presented by Simone Vierne (Grenoble: Glénat, 1986). Moreover, in the last few years, several articles have been devoted to *Jeanne*, especially to its place among Sand's pastoral novels and to comparisons between *Jeanne* and Flaubert's *Un coeur simple*.

13. I use "liberal" in the nineteenth-century sense of opposed to the monarchy, for political and civil liberties, and representing the interests of the disenfranchised but rising middle-class.

14. Mostly through references to his lack of control of discourse, which in the context of the novel, becomes a positive sign, as all discourse turns out to be patriarchal discourse.

15. As a contrast, Jeanne's friend Claudie will later be described solely in terms of her being the object of male desire. She is "appétissante" (appetizing), p. 46.

16. Sand uses the word "maîtresse" (mistress) after that of "servantes" to describe their dual role. The juxtaposition of the two underlines the irony of the term "mistress" as applied to a woman engaged in sexual relations with her "master."

17. Sand uncannily suggests the pattern of oppression which Gayle Rubin described so well in her well-known essay "The Traffic in Women. Notes on the Political Economy of Sex" (Pp. 157-210 in Rayna R. Reiter, ed. *Toward an Anthropology of Women*. New York: Monthly Review Press, 1975) in which she analyzed how the circulation of women as "gifts" for the preservation of kinship relations has been predicated upon their position as objects rather than as subject or receiver.

18. Singing is presented as a linguistic area where the peasant can express her own culture. When Jeanne is later fired from the Boussac household, she sees her return to the country as the possibility of being herself again: "She would dare sing without fear to be heard by the bourgeois" (234). Here again, Sand links music to a space where disenfranchised women can claim a certain control.

19. Her father is briefly alluded to. He was a soldier of Napoleon and died before she was born.

20. Of course, Sir Arthur is an avatar of Sir Ralph in *Indiana*, another outsider whose function is to unsettle strict gender boundaries.

21. In her study of *Jeanne, La petite Fadette*, and *Nanon*, Nancy E. Rogers ("Sand's Peasant Heroines: From Victim to Entrepreneur, From "Connaissance" to "Idée," From *Jeanne* to *Nanon*" *NCFS* 24 (1996): 347-60) argues that the heroines have "a kind of strength that others in their world term 'masculine'. Gentle Jeanne, for example, is described as 'Forte comme un homme/strong like a man!'" (337). However, Rogers does not notice that this comment is made by Marcillat along with a number of other obnoxious remarks that dehumanize Jeanne—he refers to her is "ceci" and that Marcillat is certainly not "in her world." The same passage also recounts Cadet's comment. Cadet does belong to Jeanne's world; he is a simple minded boy from Jeanne's village who comments "c'est la fille la plus forte que j'asse pas counaissue. Elle lève six boisseaux de blé et alle se les fiche sur l'épaule aussi lestement que moi, foi d'houme! Ah! la belle fille que ça fait!/ she be the strongest girl I know. She can lift them bushels of wheat and put them on her shoulders as quick as me, I'm telling you as a man, ah! what a beautiful girl she is!" (208). Sand uses the contrast between the masculine oppressor Marcillat and the disenfranchised Cadet to further question the association of force and the masculine, and she definitely refuses to masculinize Jeanne.

22. Her established strength may seem to be in contradiction with her jumping off the window, but as a careful analysis of the scene will later show, she does not jump because of fear of being attacked.

23. Ironically, her two masculine protagonists show signs of weakness. Boussac's illness is presented as a nervous illness (in a nice reversal of the stereotype that associates "nerves" with women), and Marcillat relies so much on his verbal ability because, as we have seen, he might not be a match to peasant women. Sand is thus able to demonstrate that what makes the men strong is their position within the patriarchal system, not any natural physical characteristics.

24. For instance, Isabelle Hoog Naginski mentions that Jeanne wants "to protect her virginity" (44).

25. Although her ability to defend herself against an attack by Marcillat has been well established, some readers may wonder why she did not use her strength to fight him and leave. A ready answer lies in Jeanne's inability to use violence against anyone and her inferior social status that would preclude any thought of assault on a superior.

26. Marcillat himself says "Arrière la brutale violence! C'est le fait des butors qui ne savent pas mettre la ruse et l'éloquence, l'esprit et le mensonge au service de leurs passions/No need for brutal force! Only louts resort to it because they don't know how to put cunning and eloquence, wit and lies at the service of their passions" (242). When he sees that it will be harder to convince Jeanne than he anticipated, he adds "c'est un plaidoyer, c'est un duel, et

ne pas triompher, c'est succomber/ it is like a courtroom argument, a duel, not to overcome would be to succumb" (242).

CHAPTER III
ROMANTIC NARRATIVE AUTHORITY
IN JEOPARDY
HORACE, VALVEDRE,
AND *MADEMOISELLE LA QUINTINIE*

Sand's questioning of Romantic narrative authority and her exploration both of the possibility of a female voice and of the price paid by women for internalizing male Romantic models is most visible in *Horace* (1841), *Valvèdre* (1861), and *Mlle la Quintinie* (1863). As Nigel Harkness has reminded us, Sand's reliance on male narrators is well-known[1], but what has not been analyzed is the use to which she puts such narrators to sap the very values they represent.

Horace is an example of the complexity of narrative structures in her works and of her manipulation of male first person narrators. As Scott Simpkins has asked about *Mauprat*, one must wonder how the narrative

structure of *Horace*, which is told by a male first person narrator, allows
Sand to let surge a feminine voice. First, as Dale Bauer has demonstrated
in her feminist critique of Bakhtinian dialogic, the novel reveals the
cultural restrictions that limit the possibilities of representing the "Other"
be it a member of the working class or women. Indeed in *Horace*, the
narration begins by stressing the power of the patriarchal voice at both the
diegetic and the extradiegetic level. In the extradiegetic material, George
Sand, the implied author coded as masculine, addresses a dedication and a
preface to a reader also coded as masculine. The dedication to her friend
Charles Duvernet reveals a complicity among the members of a masculine
community. The author interprets for a privileged reader (i.e., Duvernet)
the narrative to follow as a parody of a kind of man about whom George
Sand says "Nous les avons aimés quand même/Still we loved them" (25).
This "nous" could not be clearer in what it includes and what it excludes.

The foreword then broadens the scope from the male community
to readers in general, that is male readers although, as is well known, the
main readership for novels in the nineteenth-century was mostly women.
The goal of the foreword is to counteract the effect of the novel on those
readers who felt targeted by the description of the character Horace when
the novel was first published in serial form.[2] To say "ce livre m'a fait une
douzaine d'ennemis bien conditionnés/this book made me a dozen solid
enemies" is to suggest that the implied author is on an equal footing with
those offended readers since the author's representation of the male
character is so well done that some readers have completely identified with
the character. When the implied author adds "Je n'ai rien prouvé; on ne
prouve rien avec des contes, ni même avec des histoires vraies; mais les
bonnes gens ont leur conscience qui les rassure, et c'est pour eux surtout
que j'ai écrit ce livre/I did not prove anything; you do not prove anything
with tales, nor with true stories, but honest people have their conscience to
comfort them and it is for them in particular that I wrote this book" (24),
it becomes apparent that these hostile readers are only the flip side of a
patriarchal community to which the narrative is really directed. Besides

reinforcing the authority of the implied author, the goal of this notice is to veil the didactic aspect, or rather the ideological aspect of the narration, a narration which is the traditional way to reinforce patriarchal authority. At the same time the notice focuses attention on the character Horace and on criticisms of his personality while obfuscating the issue of the narrative mode and the status of the narrator himself, an effacement, which as we shall see, is of significant importance.

The narrator starts with general comments on love and friendship between men in which he addresses the reader directly. The effect of this introduction is to underline once more the complicity between the narrator and the reader, to present the story as a man's story where women are secondary or even excluded, and to affirm the narrative authority of the masculine I. This authority is reinforced throughout the narration via a first person narrator who is also an omniscient narrator as well as a key character. This omniscience is underlined in several instances by the narrator when he attempts to explain how he is able to report on conversations which he did not attend. For instance "J'ai dit ces détails de son intérieur, quoique je n'y aie point pénétré à cette époque; mais tout ce qui tient aux personnes dont je raconte ici l'histoire m'a été peu à peu dévoilé par elles-mêmes avec tant de précision, que je puis les suivre dans les circonstances de leur vie/I gave these details about her house although I had not visited it at the time; but I have been told everything relating to the people whose story I am narrating here but these persons with such precision that I can follow them in the circumstances of their life" (409).

The voice of patriarchal authority continues to be heard: besides the narrator's story, the novel moves forward through the use of dialogues between the two male characters: the narrator Théophile and the title character Horace, dialogues from which the voice of female characters is excluded. For instance, Eugénie, the narrator's companion, a Saint-Simonian seamstress to whom the narrator often refers in complimentary terms, is given voice only in the seventh chapter. Her exclusion is reinforced at the narrative level through the narrator's comments about the influence that Romanticism has had on him and on Horace. This influence is described in terms of a common tradition through which the male characters apprehend events in general and what happens to them in particular. As the narrator tells the reader "Je ne sais point séparer dans ma mémoire les impressions poétiques de mon adolescence de la lecture de *René* et d'*Atala*/I cannot separate in my memory the poetic impressions of my adolescence from my reading of *René and Atala.*" (330). These extradiegetic comments remind us that the complicity of the sender and the receiver of the narrative is a male complicity and that writing is only possible through the exclusion of the voice of woman. This exclusion appears so forced that one can wonder why Sand attempts with such obviousness to establish the authority of the masculine voice and to insure the solidarity of the reader. Indeed the use of a male narrator may, as Simpkins has suggested, make the narrative more readily acceptable for the male reader, but the use of the other techniques just described have other causes. During the course of the novel, the male univocity of the narrator is slowly transformed first in a heteroglossia that includes the voices of different sexes and classes, then, surprisingly enough, in a merging with a female voice, which was muted at the beginning but which begins to be heard, and finally, becomes one with the narrator's voice and absorbs it.

As we have seen, the beginning of the novel is marked by the absence of direct discourse reproducing the speech of the female characters. Although their speech is absent from the narrative, the echo of that speech is quite present. The narrator, for instance, describes carefully the negative reactions that his companion Eugénie has toward Horace. These reactions which contrast with the narrator's own infatuation with Horace and are reported in such a way that the bond between the narrator and the reader is undermined, as Eugénie's reactions seem to be eminently sensible and thus seem to be the voice of these "bonnes gens" to whom the notice was addressed. For instance, the narrator confides "Sa (Horace's) présence assidue chez moi était un véritable supplice pour Eugénie. Comme toutes les personnes actives et laborieuses, elle ne pouvait avoir sous les yeux le spectacle de l'inaction prolongée, sans en ressentir un malaise qui allait jusqu'à la souffrance/His continuous presence at my house was a real torture for Eugénie. Like any active and hardworking person, she could not bear to witness the spectacle of a long-lasting idleness without feeling a discomfort that was quite painful for her" (342). This surprising comment undermines from within the authority of the narrator who chooses to present Eugénie's words through the filter of his own voice (hence his use of indirect discourse rather then direct discourse), but the content of the speech that he reports contradicts the interpretation that he himself gives of the actions and the personality of Horace. Paradoxically, the refusal to represent the speech of the female character (thus to mark it as Other, as belonging to a group considered as inferior by the reader) results in valorizing the echo of this voice that now benefits from the narrator's authority. Thus the exclusion of the female voice, which at the beginning could have appeared as part of a strategy establishing the authority of the narrator, is also a strategy to make the female voice possible and to show the weakness of a narrative authority that is based on exclusion.

The second woman character, Marthe, is presented in the same way through the positive impressions of the narrator with a minimum of direct discourse. Actually, when the narrator attempts to make Marthe speak in order to discover the secret behind the presence of the painter Arsène in her husband's café, she remains silent: "elle ne répliqua pas un mot et lorsque je voulus continuer cette conversation avec elle, elle me répondit avec un calme imperturbable/she did not reply a single word and, when I attempted to carry on the conversation, she answered with great calm" (346). Her answer is a non-answer in that she lies to him. She refuses to have her voice coopted. This exchange is not presented as a dialogue; Marthe's answer is the only element presented in direct discourse, which could signal that it is precisely the lack of equality at the narrative level which ends Marthe's speech. This example of silence shows how ambivalent it is: it can be read as a sign of victimization or as a weapon.

In a second movement, the use of dialogue is amplified and comes to include all the characters, be they men or women. The first instances of direct discourse in which Eugénie and Marthe participate are caused by the need to protect and shelter Marthe, and then by the necessity to explain her situation in order to gain the narrator's help. Here women characters are given voice only when this voice is literally theirs, when the sender and the receiver participate in a speech act that is performative. Thus Eugénie speaks when she wants to protect her friend Marthe. She tells the narrator Marthe's story in order to gain his support, at the material level, which she gains since he gives her his monthly pension to help Marthe, and at the discursive level since after Eugénie's narrative about Marthe's plight, the narrator switches to direct discourse in reporting a speech that Eugénie makes about the superiority of women's love.

The abnormality of this discursive situation which is now dominated by the women characters is both underlined and denied by the report of Horace's reaction to Eugénie's speech: "Où diable prend-elle tout ce qu'elle dit? observait Horace. Mon cher, tu la laisses trop aller au prêche de la salle Taibout/Where on earth does she hear all she says? observed Horace. My dear fellow, you allow her to attend the lectures of the Taibout hall all too often." (363). In other words, according to Horace, who is the type of the young Romantic bourgeois, and perhaps according to the implied reader, what Eugénie says can only come from another masculine authority, be it a Saint-Simonian authority as the mention of Enfantin's preach at the salle Taibout suggests.

The otherness of the woman's voice that is presented is immediately negated in a movement that still aims at preserving the complicity of the masculine reader but this task is now given to one of the male characters (a most untrustworthy one at that) rather than to the narrator whose role will become increasingly the role of a double agent.

First, he will keep his role as guardian of the patriarchal voice, mostly through direct appeals to the reader such as "Pardonnez-moi, cher lecteur, de n'avoir pas songé plus tôt à vous le dire/Forgive me, dear reader,

for having failed to mention it earlier" (380) and "Dirai-je toute ma pensée
à cet égard? Je le dois à la vérité/Should I express my thoughts completely
in this regard? I must for truth's sake" (385) and through comments
making light of Eugénie's negative reactions to Horace in order to justify
him. Secondly and paradoxically, the constant efforts of the narrator to
justify the weaknesses of Horace are accompanied by general reflections
that imply the opposite of these justifications. These reflections could
easily come from Eugénie, both at the level of form and content. That is,
the narrator's idiolect is also that of the female character. We have here a
narrative situation where the narrator is the spokesperson for the female
characters while appearing to support the point of view of Horace, the male
character who represents the most exaggerated aspect of patriarchal and
Romantic ideology.

The similarity between the voice of the narrator and that of
Eugénie is not caused by an authorial inability to differentiate between
voices because the voices of the other characters are clearly marked.
Horace's voice, for instance, is full of Romantic clichés and passion, that
of the working-class sisters of Arsène is marked by provincialisms and
barbarisms underlining their lack of education and vulgar spirit; the
aristocratic characters such as the Comtesse de Chailly speak in a language
studded with pretentious expressions meant to be poetic. The ridiculous
and inauthentic aspect of these expressions is stressed at the narrative level
through the use of italics both in the description of the aristocratic milieu
and in the dialogues involving upper class characters. This clear separation
of voices signals a heteroglossia marking, in particular, differences of
social class. Indeed, the main characters—the narrator, Eugénie, and
Marthe--seem all to speak in the same voice. Although the two women
come from modest backgrounds and are "grisettes" they use a language
that is as sophisticated as that of the narrator who is an educated bourgeois.
They even use the *passé simple*, a literary tense reserved for narration.

The similarity between the voice of the female protagonists and the
narrator's voice can be analyzed and clarified through the use of

narratological distinctions that Susan Lanser has established between public and private narration. By public narration, she means narration that is addressed to a narratee who is external to the text: here the narrate is a public supposedly composed of male readers. On the other hand, private narration is aimed at a narratee expressly named in the text and who exists only in the text so that the reader only has indirect access to the narrative. Thus the similarity between the female voice and the narrator's voice can be seen as the trace of a private narration aimed at an implied narratee who would be separate from the patriarchal audience, women for instance. In *Horace* everything seems to belong to the realm of public narration and to establish a relation of authority between different members of the patriarchal order, but the amalgamation of the feminine voice and the narrator's voice does not belong to this public narrative structure. On the contrary it suggests the presence of a private narrative structure where the narrative act is possible only through the appropriation of the woman's voice by the narrator. The narrative ,in the end, is not Marthe's narrative; it is that of the way in which the narrator narrates and of the price paid to obtain his narrative. Marthe's story, that is her victimization at the hands of her father, then of her husband, and most importantly of her lover Horace, is possible mostly because the narrator insists on forcing Horace into the life of the female characters. Here the narrative structure coincides with the socio-cultural context, which does not allow for a direct change in the situation of women at the level of institutions: the structure of public narration can only remain and Sand must operate at the level of private narration. The blending of the narrator's voice and the female voice expresses the conditions for the existence of the feminine voice, that is, it must remain clandestine and implicit for it to be heard at all. Public narration leaves intact the hegemonic structures of writing but it is undermined from within by the private narration which no longer addresses male-identified readers, but rather female-identified readers a narrative quite different from the one presented at the public narration level. It is the narrative of the strategies that must be put in place to allow a feminine voice to surge within a context of patriarchal narration.

Twenty years later, Sand will write again the story of the emerging female voice but while she will still use a male-identified first person narrator, the structure of public narration is longer stable. On the contrary, her displacement of Romantic male-identified narrative authority will be more systematic and more obvious. She will show that the cultural devaluation and exclusion of the feminine is directly linked to the failure of patriarchal structures.

Valvèdre ,which Sand wrote in the Spring of 1861 at the age of 57 years, offers a scathing critique of Romantic conceptions of love and women as well as a contestation of cultural authority as it is specifically expressed in narrative authority. This novel deserves to be placed among the greatest texts authored by Sand and major nineteenth-century novels. Yet after two reeditions in the 1860's, and an unusually positive comment by Henry James, it has yet to be rediscovered and given the kind of attention it deserves.

The novel is framed by a dedication to Sand's son Maurice and by a preface which explains the origin of the novel. Both are crucial because they undermine the voice of the first narrator whom Sand uses throughout the novel to present the characters. In the preface, Sand links the novel to scientific work; both express an interest in the study of nature and the idea behind the work of the scientist and the writer is to turn outward ("sortir de soi") to break with the long tradition of "Man thinking he is the center of the universe" (1). This exploration of the universe can be achieved through the study of science as well as literature, by a young man or an older woman. In other words, such a quest is inclusive and the preface itself is an example of turning outward as is Maurice Sand's own scientific study[3]. Even before the novel starts and the narrator begins writing, Sand has undermined his method since he is presented as someone incapable of going beyond himself. He describes two ways of writing: 1. representation of a real place (which he rejects), 2. vaguer description to communicate received impressions (which he adopts). Unfortunately for his credibility, he admits his own confusion about the places he recalls: they seemed either splendid or miserable according to his mood (in good Romantic fashion) although the avowed goal of his travels to Switzerland and Italy was the "need to see and understand life in general" (4).

Thus from the start, the authority of the Romantic narrator, although he is seemingly given the control of the narrative, is undermined by the author. However, Sand is careful to make the narrator attractive both to hold the reader's interest and to express the attraction that Romanticism had held and continued to hold. We learn that the narrator (who remains nameless until much later when a female character introduces him as Francis Valigny to another female character), is an aspiring poet with a book of anonymous verse to his credit who is doing his grand tour and who, at the insistence of his parents, goes to see his childhood friend, Henry Obernay, a Swiss citizen and botanist who is the son of a distinguished scientist and pedagogue. Obernay is in the Alps working with another scientist named Valvèdre who is off exploring mountains. At the inn where they are staying, the narrator meeets a rich Jewish business man named Moserwald who gossips about Valvèdre and his wife, a topic who becomes the center of several conversations the narrator has with Moserwald and Obernaï. Mme Valvèdre arrives unexpectedly with Paule, Valvèdre's sister who is engaged to Obernaï. The narrator falls in love with Alida Valvèdre, a beautiful woman who feels abandoned by her husband and who both shares and embodies the narrator's Romantic beliefs about passion and women. The novel registers the narrator's complicated involvement with Mme Valvèdre who reciprocates his attachment but who insists on keeping the relationship platonic. With the help of Moserwald, himself hopelessly in love with Mme Valvèdre, the narrator and Alida Valvèdre finally elope and live platonically while waiting for her husband to give her a divorce, as is permitted under Swiss Protestant law. Before this can happen, the narrator, who can neither support himself nor her, borrows money from Moserwald and moves her to Northern Africa as her health declines (the fumes of Paris are deadly, it would seem). This relation, still platonic, makes the two lovers unhappy; among other things, Alida Valvèdre is depressed at having left her children while the narrator fights against his awareness that her husband is a superior human being and that he has made a terrible mistake. But it would seem that all's well that ends well: Alida dies after being forgiven by her husband; the narrator is thus freed from his burden, spends the next seven years working in a metallurgic factory, after which time Obernai calls him back to tutor one of Valvèdre's sons. The narrator ends up marrying one of Obernai's sisters while he plays Cupid to Obernai's other sister Adelaide and Valvèdre.

The narrative of this ill-fated affair allows Sand to question Romantic representations of the female subject and to expose the disastrous consequences such notions of femininity have for both the male narrator and the female character. She shows that when women internalize traditional patriarchal discourses and expectations about femininity, they are doomed, while the women characters who, for a reason or another, do not fit nineteenth-century conventions of womenhood live happy, contented lives. The function of the narrator as a type is clearly established: although he explains his position as a young poet suffering from "la maladie du siècle, l'ennui, le doute, l'orgueil/the illness of the century, boredom, doubt, arrogance" (11), he does not give us his name. Although he, self-servingly, opposes his Romanticism to lack of ideals and greed, his opposite is Obernai who pursues the study of nature, and of the laws of the universe. Obernai is the same age as the narrator but he is very energetic and an example of someone who can go beyond himself, turn outward, as Sand had stated in the preface. The description of Obernai, by its opposition to that of the narrator, suggests that there are many ways of being a "man" (which by extension will become there are many ways of being a woman). Obernai is physically strong but his strength is the result of exercise, not of his "organization." His skin is smooth and white and, as the narrator notices, could be envied by a woman. In other words, Obernai has male characterics which are the result of a practice (or a performance). Before analyzing the narrator's representation of woman as female-Other, as a creature of feelings, as a hybrid, as medusa, it is interesting to note that the few details he gives us about himself suggest the precariousness of his own position on the gender scale since he is short (his size is contrasted to Obernai's strength) and half-Spanish through his mother (20). In other words he is himself a hybrid. These details added to the preface contribute to make the readers suspicious of the narrator's presentation.

The narrator's mode of presentation of Alida Valvèdre indicates by its indirectness the complex mediation through which "woman" is apprehended. First, he hears about her through the gossip of Moserwald (who reports that she is a beautiful woman sacrificed to an original (18)). Moserwald's comments are followed by a number of vulgar jokes that would seem to discredit his views. The narrator seeks Obernai's opinion; and Obernai reveals that he doesn't think well of Alida Valvèdre because of her lack of energy and her lack of intellect. She is "nonchalante et fatiguée comme une créole/indolent and tired like a Creole" (34). She has "une âme sans énergie, un cerveau sans étendue, un caractère inégal, irritable et mou; aucune aptitude sérieuse et de sots dédains pour ce qu'elle ne comprend pas/a soul without energy, a brain without breadth, an uneven, irritable and weak character; no gift for anything and a silly scorn for the things that she does not understand" (34-35). In this harsh description, Obernai adds that she is the daughter of a Swede and a Spaniard; in other words she is very much like the narrator. These similarities, of course, are not perceived by the narrator, but they already suggest that gender differences are not a matter of binary opposites; rather they belong to a sliding scale that allows distanciation. Later in the novel, Obernai's sisters will analyze the reasons for Alida's lack of energy and intellect and make clear that it has nothing to do with her "nature" or her "predisposition." They blame her parents and their decision not to educate her.

Before the narrator actually meets Mme Valvèdre, he dreams about her. This dream indicates that woman for the narrator (and metonymically for the Romantics) is a fantasy created through the discourse of other men and through the narrator's need to exclude from his consciousness his own uncertainty about his masculinity. The presence in his dream of Moserwald whom he calls "the Jew" and who is the man who spoke to him about Mme Valvèdre reinforces this interpretation. The dream is followed by the narrator's admission that he feels a predisposition to love her (even though he hasn't met her yet) "je croyais beaucoup à la fatalité. C'était la mode en ce temps là, et croire à la fatalité, c'est la créer en nous-même/I believed in fate. It was fashionable at that time, and to believe in fate is to create it within ourselves." (35) As the older, wiser narrator seems to acknowledge, it is his fantasy that is fatality.

When the narrator finally sees Mme Valvèdre on his way back from a walk in the Alps, he doesn't know who she is. Because he does not know the identity of the woman at whom he is looking, his impression is curiously free of Romantic stereotypes about seduction. He notices her "oeil noir étrange et assez effrayant/strange and rather frightening black eye" (39) and his reaction is negative "Elle ne me plaisait pas. Elle me paraissait maigre et colorée...Son regard était dur et sa voix aussi/I did not like her. She seemed thin and ruddy...Her gaze was harsh and so was her voice." (39) He is afraid of the woman he doesn't know but as soon as he meets her in circumstances where a Romantic scenario can be envisaged, his description changes: fear and desire now mix; however, what remains the same is the fact that what he describes is not Mme Valvèdre but her effect on him and his desire. Throughout the novel, the narrator's descriptions indicate that the woman he observes and then loves is at a distance, is a mystery: "Elle me *paraissait* maigre/She seemed thin to me" [emphasis mine] (41), "je l'avais imaginée/I had imagined her" (46), "elle m'avait paru/she had seemed to me" (49), "elle sembla se laisser aller/she seemed to let herself go" (89), etc. Thus the character of Alida Valvèdre is reduced to being the object of his Romantic love.

When he describes their first full encounter, her beauty is analyzed in terms of power, struggle, indeterminacy, and physical effects: "Ce regard de femme fut si expressif que je le sentis passer en moi, de la tête aux pieds, comme un frisson brûlant/This woman's gaze was so expressive that I felt it go through me, from head to toe, like a burning shiver." (43). The characterization of her gaze as a "Woman's" gaze reveals not so much the reason for her seductive power but that his desire is triggered by his finding an object who fits his expectations about what a woman is. For the Romantic narrator, femininity is what engages his desire, and, as earlier comments make clear, femininity refers not to what woman is, but to how she acts in order to please men (i.e., it is a performance). This point is emphasized by the narrator's previous comment about Paule's, (Obernai's fiancée and Valvèdre's sister)lack of femininity as she fails to freshen up before her appearing before her fiancé and the narrator, who comments "Elle n'était pas assez femme/She was not womanly enough" (45).

The rest of the narrator's description uses all the negative characteristics attached to essential womanhood in order to stress Alida Valvèdre's power and her mystery—for instance her gaze is a "puissance mystérieuse/mysterious power" (43), her eye "une ombre changeante, n'était ni bleu, ni noir, ni verdâdre, ni orangé/a changing shadow, neither blue nor black nor green or gold" (48)...toutes les angoisses du désir ou toutes les défaillances de la volupté passaient dans l'âme dont il voulait s'emparer/all the pangs of desire or all the weakness of pleasure went through the soul it sought to conquer" (48), "n'osant plus regarder son visage, persuadé que je perdrais l'esprit...J'étais comme noyé dans les parfums de sa robe et de ses cheveu/no longer daring to look at her face, convince that I was losing my mind...I was like engulfed in the scent of her dress and of her hair" (49), and finally "ce vêtement dont émanait un fluide embrasé qui m'empêchait de respirer et de parler/this dress which exuded a burning liquid that prevented me from breathing and from speaking." (49) However, the narrator's presentation of woman as a dangerous, unknowable Medusa uncovers the projection of his own desire. The power of the woman's bewitching gaze is one of the Romantic myths which the novel questions. Later when Obernai's sister Adelaide is introduced to the narrator he is warned not to stare at her because Adelaide's great beauty causes her to be the constant object of the gaze of strangers, which is a great source of embarrassment and pain. The contrast between the two versions of the gaze is striking: the male version, which is the dominant version in nineteenth-century literary discourse, emphasizes the unavoidable and dangerous power of the woman's eye, while the female version expresses the pain felt under the aggression of male desire. Even Alida Valvèdre, who, as we shall see, shares the narrator's Romantic views on love and women, assesses the narrator's interpretation. She tells him "vous subissez une très vive émotion auprès de moi, mais croyez-vous que la force de votre désir vous crée un mérite quelconque?/you are feeling a very strong emotion when you are with me, but do you think that the strength of your desire makes you worthy in any way?" (105). In other words, the Romantic discourse on women that emphasizes their power and their mystery operates a displacement: what is mysterious and powerful is the force of men's own desire, and as Sand's preface stated, man's inability to "go beyond himself," as the preface advocated.

As a contrast to the Romantic narcissistic gaze, Sand presents secondary characters like Obernai and Paule who, when they are together, indulge in botany, their common passion. What they look at is not each other's eyes but flowers that they inventory. Thus the novel shows that the dynamics of the gaze promoted by Romantic ideology is not an inescapable one; the alternate version acted out by the secondary characters gives more autonomy to both sexes.

Similarly, the Romantic narrator's attempts to make the woman responsible for his infatuation through his repeated use of words suggesting that she possesses an irrational power, words like "magicienne" (49), "charme, enchanteresse/charm, enchantress" (190), "magicienne haletante et jalouse/breathless and jealous magician" (192), etc, are quietly undermined by his own description of his meeting with the stranger who will turn out to be the magician's husband. The narrator explains that he was "poussé par un attrait inexplicable et comme condamné par une invisible puissance à m'attacher aux pas de cet homme/led by an unfathomable attraction and as if condemned by an invisible power to follow this man." (163). Here again, the narrator blames external powers for his attraction to another person. However, because the object of his attraction is male, he does not assign the power directly to him.

An alternate version of the Romantic demonization of woman is that of Valvèdre who recognizes his own responsibility in falling in love with his ill-suited wife Alida. He admits "c'est moi qui ai commis la faute en cherchant l'infini dans les yeux décevants d'une femme qui ne le comprenait pas/I was the one who made the mistake of looking for infinity in the disappointing eyes of a woman who did not understand it." (242). He too read into her his own desires and aspirations without knowing her. Alida herself gives a sharp analysis of men's so called passion both when she describes the story of their marriage and when she questions the narrator at the beginning of their relation. She warns him that what he feels is not love: "Chez les hommes, ces sortes de vouloirs sont *aveugles*/Among men, these kinds of desire are *blind*" (105). That is men's passion is basically a narcissistic desire. Her account of her marriage also blames her husband: "Je lui plus, il me trouva belle, il voulut être mon mari afin de pouvoir être mon amant. Voilà tout le mystère de ces grandes affections auxquelles une jeune fille sans expérience est condamnée à se laisser prendre/ He took a fancy to me, he found me beautiful, he wished to be my husband in order to be my lover. Here is all the mystery of these great passions by which an inexperienced young woman is condemned to be caught." (114). Although Sand uses the character of Alida to represent the dangers of Romanticism for women, it is remarkable that she also gives her powers of analysis that contrast sharply with the narrator's self-deception. What Alida knows is that being the object of men's desire means nothing in terms of their recognition of her as a subject. Her experience with her husband who fell out of love once he realized who she actually was explains her unbelievable demand that her relation with the narrator remains platonic. As the narrator has told us, Alida is an avid reader of novels; that is, she knows all too well the fate of Romantic heroines who give in to men's desires.

However, as Sand shows us, keeping men's desire a fantasy is not enough to escape the usual fate of Romantic heroines. Romanticism, even if it is in the form of platonic love is self-destructive. Not only does Sand show the underpinnings of male Romantic love but she also analyzes the inevitable consequenses of female endorsement of Romantic ideology.

First, Alida Valvèdre claims an essential nature for women; an essence that makes them creatures of love whose whole existence is to be devoted to love. As she claims "j'ai passionément aimé M. de Valvèdre. Il n'a qu'un défaut, il n'aime pas. Moi je suis une femme, une vraie femme, faible, ignorante, sans valeur aucune. Je ne sais qu'aimer/I loved Mr. Valvèdre passionately. He has only one failing. He cannot love. As for me, I am a woman, a real woman, weak, ignorant, without any value, love is the only thing I know." (114). The narrator agrees with this assessment and her need for love throughout the novel, but while her description of the essential woman seems to fit perfectly patriarchal and Romantic expectations, the readers are showed the disastrous consequenses this has. Alida demands the sole and constant attention of the man she loves. Her lofty declarations are couched in typical Romantic rhetoric "Depuis que j'existe j'aspire à l'amitié, à l'amour vrai...je cherche une affection à la fois ardente et pure; une préférence absolue, exclusive, de mon âme pour un être qui la comprenne et qui consente à la remplir sans la déchirer/From the beginning of my life, I have aspired to experience friendship, true love...I am looking for an affection both ardent and pure, an absolute, exclusive preference of my soul for someone who would understand it and consent to fill it without tearing it apart." (106). Her emphasis on love transforms the lover into a dog (97) or a slave (97), to use the expressions used by the narrator to explain his devotion; that is, the male lover loses his humanity and his freedom. Valvèdre's comments concur with the narrator's description of the role the male must play when a woman endorses with a vengeance a patriarchal Romantic notion of womanhood. As Alida has stated "On ne m'a pas appris à travailler...Je suis une femme: ma destinée est d'aimer mon mari et d'élever mes enfants/I was not taught to work. I am a woman: my destiny is to love my husband and to bring up my children." (254), "Aimer est tout..et celui qui aime n'a pas le temps de s'occuper d'autre chose/Love is everything and a person who loves has time for nothing else" (253), which means that in order to please her Valvèdre had to abandon his research "Je me fis son esclave, je me fis enfant avec elle, je cachai les livres, je renonçai presque à l'étude./I made myself her slave, I became childlike with her, I hid my books, I almost gave up my work." (246). Thus when women like Alida internalize a patriarchal essentialist discourse that assigns an inferior status to women, the consequenses are devastating for themselves as well as for their male companions, whose ability to work is diminished. The husband had to temporarily give up his research, the narrator with whom she elopes doesn't find the time to write in order to take care of her. The adoption of Romantic ideology translates into an incapacity to work for both sexes.

This inability to produce meaningful work is presented as an illness. When Obernai's sisters discuss Alida and the reasons for her boredom and unhappiness, they mention the fact that her parents did not want her to be educated and that (220), as a result, she cannot focus nor think with direction; she is idle and doesn't want to learn although she is quite intelligent. Adelaide, who, as we shall see, is presented by the implied author as a version of an "ideal" woman, describes Alida's state as a "maladie très douloureuse et dont on guérirait par l'étude des choses vraies/quite painful illness from which one would recover through the study of true things." (221); this could be language from the author's preface. Alida suffers from the same illness as the narrator except that in her case, lack of education and traditional views of the role of women seem to explain, if not justify, her idleness whereas the narrator has no such justification.

Alida's self proclaimed essential femininity (she refers to herself as a "true woman" on at least two occasions (236, 255) and so does the narrator), her focus on love and physical beauty—what the narrator calls "l'art féminin grâce auquel sa beauté pâlie et fatiguée rivalisait avec les plus luxuriantes jeunesses/the feminine art thanks to which her faded and tired beauty rivaled that of the most luxuriant youths" (236), not only has negative consequenses for the men who subscribe to her views but it also affects her relations with her children. Her first pregancy accentuated her jealousy and instability. When her husband recounts his life to Obernay he notes "j'étais assez médecin pour savoir que la grossesse est quelquefois accompagnée d'une sorte d'insanité d'esprit. Je redoublais de soumission, d'effacement, de soins/I was enough of a doctor to know that pregnancy is sometimes accompanied by a kind of insanity of mind. I increased my submissiveness, my self-effacement, my care." (247). His submission and his medical knowledge cannot prevent her jealousy of the nurse who takes care of her child when Alida is unable to do it herself because she is sick. Interestingly her husband's explanations emphasize Alida's state of physical weakness and her refusal to observe basic rules of hygiene. The scientist Valvèdre is not refering to her lacking any kind of maternal instinct but to physical and psychological strength as well as to a body of knowledge necessary to be a fit mother. As a woman and a Romantic heroine who dismisses work and learning, Alida cannot be a mother although she claims that her destiny is to bring up her children (255); her internalization of Romantic gender ideals prevent her from fulfilling that destiny. Valvèdre himself tells her that she is not "une mère intelligente/an intelligent mother," that is, a mother who can help her children grow up and become stronger. Motherhood (that is successful motherhood) is presented here as incompatible with Romantic ideals though these ideals seem to confine women to the very role of lover, wife and mother.

Sand's reconsideration of motherhood and her deglamorization of giving birth is further clarified by Valvèdre's final comment on the subject when Alida proves unable to take care of her children "J'enseignai à ma soeur ainée la **science** des mères que ma femme ne voulait pas acquérir/I taught my older sister the science of motherhood that my wife did not want to learn" (26). Motherhood is thus a science, a body of acquired knowledge[4] rather that some irrational, instinctual characteristic of women. Valvèdre's sister Juste is unmarried and without children of her own, details which emphasize all the more a version of motherhood as a performance needing skills and knowledge. The use of the expression "science des mères" is not to be discredited because it is used by a male scientist (and because it could thus be seen as belonging to the nineteenth-century oppressive medical discourse on women) since Valvèdre is presented as a superior human who has used his medical knowledge to save a shepherd's child (126); in fact it takes us back to Sand's prefacial address to her own son where she advocates the ideal of "sortir de soi," i.e., the deliberate attempt to be engaged with the outside world. Motherhood, as she conceives of it, is such an attempt. In *Valvèdre* Sand both unveils the contradictions present in Romantic views of women and motherhood and reconfigures motherhood as something that needs to be part of women's knowledge of the world.

However, her representation of motherhood as knowledge is not used to vilify Alida as the figure of the bad mother; Sand just shows that natural affection is not enough. Alida cares for her sons, at least, for the older one (she can't bear the thought of her oldest son going away to study (160)), and the biggest remorse she feels after eloping with the narrator is to have abandoned her children and not be able to see them. Alida is not presented as a monster: her pain and regrets are real. She embodies the split required of women when they adopt an essentializing stance defined by men. As a contrast, the characters whom Alida derides as "femmes savantes" (i.e., Obernai's sisters) are all "good" mothers. Adelaide's tutoring of her younger sister is described as "maternal solicitude" (233) and Obernai's wife, Paule, will not be apart from her children (326). Sand has rewritten with a twist the nineteenth-century cultural images that collide notions of womanhood and motherhood with a patriarchal version of women as essentially ignorant creatures. In *Valvèdre* old maids and educated young women make the best mothers. She also reveals the price women like Alida pay for their ignorance and their allegiance to male Romantic ideals: they cannot succeed as mothers and their love affairs leave them unhappy and unfulfilled.

One recurrent theme which runs through the representation of Alida as a woman who internalizes patriarchal discourses and expectations about femininity is that of the woman as child. All of the characters commenting of Alida's personality note her childlike qualities. These comments range from the narrator's "Mme de Valvèdre était une séduisante enfant qu'il fallait toujours occuper et distraire pour l'arracher à une mélancholie profonde/Mrs. Valvèdre was an attractive child that one had to occupy constantly and to entertain in order to rescue her from a deep melancholy." (100) to Paule's "Alida est bonne, elle a du coeur. A beaucoup d'égard, c'est une enfant/Alida is good, kind. In many respects, she is a child." (112) to Valvèdre who reports telling her "Ma pauvre chère enfant, vous êtes dévorée par votre imagination et vous dévorez tout autour de vous/My poor dear child, you are consumed by your imagination and you consume everything that is around you" (255). These comments all imply that being like a child is a cause of unhappiness for her as well as for others. Interestingly enough, the narrator whose views of women require that they are like children unwittingly registers the high cost of such childishness. He states "je ne trouvais pas en elle ce fond de logique, cette maturité de l'esprit, cette conscience de la volonté qui sont les indispensables bases d'une affection bienfaisante et d'une intimité heureuse/I did not find in her the logical grounding, the maturity, the consciousness of the will that are the indispensable bases of a beneficent affection and of a happy intimacy." (166), to which he adds the telling "elle était femme jusqu'au bout des ongles/She was all woman" (116). In these remarks the narrator links essential femininity and childishness while the other characters deplore Alida's child-like characteristics as traits that prevent her from leading a happy life. The narrator's position (i.e., she is a woman, therefore she is like a child) is undermined by his own recognition of the qualities necessary for a lasting relation. His conception of love and women conflicts with any possibility of a successful relationship. Sand seems to suggest that holding the view that women are and should be child-like creatures is itself a sign of immaturity and narcissism. Not too subtly, she even has the narrator refer to himself as a child when he expresses his surprise that Alida would need "la protection d'un enfant (that is, himself) qu'elle voyait pour la première fois/the protection of a child whom she saw for the first time" (89). Here Sand reiterates her view of the Romantic lover as a narcissistic child, a theme developed in *Lucrezia Floriani, Horace*, and *Gabriel* among others. Of course, if Romantic views of love and women express male narcissism, it is obvious that women who internalize these views are bound to be destroyed as Alida is.

But Alida is no Emma Bovary. Beside being beautiful, she is intelligent, articulate, and pure, an aspect of her character for which Sand happily sacrifices vraisemblance. Unlike her male counterparts, Sand creates a woman character who dies, not because of her weaknesses as a woman, but because she has embraced all too readily patriarchal constructions of femininity, because she is trapped in a narrow conception of gender based on binary opposites. Through Alida's story, Sand shows the inadequacy of binaries, be they gender or race binaries. Indeed one of the least attractive aspects of Alida is her antisemitism and her scornful attitude toward Moserwald. While the Moserwald subplot may seem only loosely related to Alida's story, it is central to the thematic core of the novel: i.e., the inadequacy of binaries and of exclusion to conceptualize human beings. Again, Alida takes to an extreme the prejudices expressed by the male characters and by doing so serves to demonstrate that they are just prejudices. Although the narrator describes Moserwald patronizingly and considers himself quite different from him, Moserwald claims as his own the very *mal du siècle* that aches the narrator and is in love with the same woman. Moreover, although the narrator and Alida reject Moserwald's vulgar and naive conception of love as something that can be

How does this shed the interconnected men of all prejudices?
* * Are all prejudices interconnected?

110   *Narrative Authority*

bought with jewels, money, or charm, they both end up living off loans Moserwald gives the narrator and meeting in a house that belongs to him. In a twist that reveals the interconnectedness of all prejudices, be they gender or race prejudices, the very character that is categorically rejected by Alida is the one who makes possible the realization of her Romantic desires (i.e., of her prejudices about women's roles). Moreover, Moserwald,[5] who knows the material and legal conditions that control the lovers' fate, predicts the main developments of the plot (that Alida and the narrator will elope, that Alida is not married according to the dictates of the Catholic church—therefore she can divorce; that Valvèdre will end up loving Adélaide).

Sand links Alida's conception of essential femininity to her religious beliefs, i.e., her Catholicism and her sense of sin. This connection between Alida's belief in Romantic notions of love and women as well as her allegiance to the dictates of the Catholic church are not contradictory since both are expressions of a patriarchal structure that limits women's autonomy and are based on a denial of their rationality. In the early stage of her relation with the narrator, Alida uses a language heavy with religious rhetoric "Quand le coeur est adultère, le devoir est déja trahi; je ne me fais pas d'illusion sur moi-même/When the heart is adulterous, duty is already betrayed. I do not have any illusions about myself." (151). When the narrator intends to break up with Alida in the early stages of their relation, he follows her to the church where she has taken refuge to pray, and he is seduced again: "elle était si saisissante et si belle dans son voluptueux accablement/she was so striking and so beautiful in her voluptuous despondency." (197). Thus the church and Romantic desire are linked metonymically and symbolically in their common support of women's ignorance and the exaltation of the affective domain at the expense of rationality. Moreover Alida refuses the narrator's offer to marry her after she separates from her husband because she accepts the absolute authority of the chuch and the dogma of the indissolubility of marriage. Of course, having Alida endorse the dictates of the Catholic church is the best way for

Sand to discredit such a position, since Alida herself has registered the failure of her marriage, her awareness of her breach of duty and her general unhappiness, not to mention the fact that her husband no longer loves her and that she has abandoned her children. Sand's distrust of the church's role in the subjection of women and of the alliance of women with the church is not original: it inscribes itself in the French post revolutionary tradition that long denied women political and civil rights because they were associated with the conservative power of the Catholic church.[6] What is original is that, rather than just rejecting women as the pawns of the church, through a depiction of their subjection under the church as well as under Romantic rhetoric, she shows the links between religious and Romantic ideology.

Sand shows that the cultural construction of woman as an essential creature, a creature of feelings, is embedded in a structure that is religious, social as well as aesthetic. The narrator and Alida's espousal of Romantic ideals are linked to the aesthetic of art for art's sake, which is opposed, in the preface and throughout the novel, to an art that is engaged with the outside world. Here again Sand is rejecting the Romantic exclusive reliance on inner feelings. The narrator (and of course the readers) note Alida's self-absorbtion and her control of language. He remarks on her "analyse excessive de sa personnalité/excessive analysis of her personality" (153)which he admits he shares as "le moi tenait une place démesurée dans mes réflections comme dans mes instincts/the ego held an inordinate place in my thoughts and in my instincts." (153) He emphasizes Alida's powerful rhetoric both in her speech and in her letters, which are "ravissantes/gorgeous" we are told (160). He admires her style "Elle avait le don d'exprimer admirablement un certain ordre d'idées. Elle avait lu beaucoup de romans; mais pour l'exaltation ou les subtilités des sentiments, elle en eût remontré aux plus habiles romanciers/She had the gift of expressing marvellously well a certain range of ideas. She had read many novels, but for the exaltation or the subtleties of feelings, she could have given lessons to the most clever novelists." (152). Indeed what is remarkable in Sand's representation of a type of woman whom she obviously rejects is her giving her an astonishing control of discourse. Alida becomes as much of a voice as the narrator; as the story progresses, it not only describes, through the narrator, Alida's control of language, but it stresses the presence of her own voice through numerous direct discourse quotes in which her voice is unmediated. Alida utters a number of stylistically striking sentences that have a classical beauty (for instance "l'outrage atteint toujours une veuve dont le mari est vivant/insults always hit a widow whose husband is still alive." (86); the function of such direct quotes is to make the reader experience the seduction of that voice even if the content expressed by the speaker is rejected at the thematic level. Sand goes beyond the trope of the misguided Romantic heroine as reader of novels; she shows a woman who is not only a reader but a producer of discourse, a discourse like that of art for art's sake, which seduces by its beauty, but is deeply narcissistic and causes the intellectual and moral demise of the utterer.

In *Valvèdre* Sand goes beyond the demonstration of the impossibility of a female voice as she had in *Horace*. What she shows is that the mastery of a type of discourse that reproduces patriarchal structures and that is based on binary divisions is destructive because it necessarily excludes part of that voice. The figure of Alida who has internalized patriarchal views of femininity, who demonstrates a patriarchal control of discourse while performing as a "pure" woman shows us the cost of such performance. However, Sand is careful not to blame Alida's death on the exterior Romantic narrator; she claims responsibility for her character. The narrator is told by his friend Obernai that the illness that affects Alida began well before his association with her. The illness is never fully explained, except for the fact that it is not physical, but rather "nervous." Sand, however, has avoided the stereotype of the woman as hysteric and has accumulated on her all the signs of depression, not a surprising state for a woman who has internalized demands that are destructive.

As a contrast to Alida's self-proclaimed status as a "vraie femme," we are presented with the character of Adélaïde who represents an alternate version of womanhood, one that seems to threaten the narrator's sense of identity and authority. The reader's first introduction to Adélaide, as we have seen earlier, occurs when her brother warns the narrator not to look at her too obviously because her beauty is a source of pain as it subjects her to the gaze of strangers. Her reaction implicitly contradicts the narrator's analysis of women as a source of bewitching power. Throughout the novel this initial contradiction will be amplified as the narrator rejects what Adélaïde represents at the same time as his enthusiastic descriptions reveal her superiority. This contrast between the representation of Adélaïde as a superior person and his irrational rejection signal his deep insecurity and his "sexism." For instance, after stating "Elle n'était pas seulement la plus belle créature qui existât peut-être à cette époque: elle était la plus docte et la plus aimable, comme la plus sage et la plus heureuse/Not only was she the most beautiful creature who may have lived at the time, but she was also the wisest, the most pleasant, the most learned and the happiest." (233), the narrator opposes her to Alida "la femme type" by adding "l'autre (i.e., Adélaïde) n'est qu'un *hybride* dénaturé par l'éducation/the other is but a hybrid perverted by education." (236). Clearly Adélaïde threatens the narrator's belief that the sexes are radically different, with ignorance and inferiority on the feminine side and knowledge and power on the other. Although Adélaïde possesses all the traits usually associated with traditional femininity—beauty, modesty, kindness—and although she should therefore appeal to the narrator as fulfilling his expectations, she is also physically strong and very accomplished both as a scientist and as an artist. The narrator calls her a "hybrid" precisely because she crosses boundaries and her existence challenges the strict binary oppositions upon which the narrator's sense of identity is built. He obviously feels that Adélaide's existence is a question put to his masculinity: it asks what kind of a man he is and what does it mean to be a man if being a woman is being like her.

The narrator's way to avoid the question is to deny that Adélaïde is a woman. He does so in two ways; first by insisting on her status as a hybrid; that is claiming that she is a "femme supérieure" (that is paradoxically not really a woman). The narrator states that Adélaïde "est une femme supérieure c'est à dire une espèce d'homme. Elle ne sera pas longtemps belle, il lui poussera de la barbe/is a superior woman, that is, a kind of man. She will not be beautiful long; she will grow a beard" (235). Of course, the narrator has trouble denying her beauty (an anchor of his definition of woman as the one who attracts men) since she is so beautiful but he can fantasize that her beauty is a temporary aberration. His ludicrous attempt to defeminize her reveals his deep anxiety in the presence of a woman who has all the physical characteristics usually associated with femininity but who is not an intellectual inferior, as if he ackowledges that the function of woman is not to be the other ("l'autre") but to represent and embody what man fears he may be (in the narrator's case, weak, ignorant, and unhappy).

The second way in which the narrator rejects Adélaïde's femininity is through his dismissal of her physicality, i.e., by denying that she can desire or be desired (if she cannot be desired by a man [i.e., him, of course], then she is not a woman; thus he is a man after all). When he recounts dancing with her (an act involving the physical presence of both partners and usually a charged erotic experience) he describes her, using a vocabulary stripping her of real physical presence: "splendide et parfaite créature...les magnificences de son divin sourire...les perfections de tout son être pudique et suave/splendid and perfect creature...the splendors of her divine smile...the perfections of her whole chaste and heavenly being." (191) The heavy use of religious vocabulary makes Adélaïde into such an ethereal, ideal creature that she is no longer human, thus no longer a woman. What is at stake for the narrator here is clear when this description is put beside a slightly earlier episode where he plays with her in the garden: "Adélaïde courait après moi avec la rapidité d'une flèche. J'avais peine à échapper à cette jeune Atalante et je m'étonnais de tant de force unie à tant de souplesse et de grâce/ran after me with the speed of a shot.

I had difficulty escaping this young Atalant and I was surprised by so much strength allied to so much suppleness and grace." (177). The narrator must dehumanize Adélaïde because her presence shatters his belief that women are physically and intellectually inferior. Moreover her strength is a challenge to what he feels is his weakness (he is not fast enough to escape her). Adélaïde's presence triggers in him a sense of lack. Even in this episode, although the narrator does acknowledge Adélaïde's physicality, his reference to her as an Atalante contributes to placing her outside the human realm into that of myths. The twist here is that in the Greek myth, the virgin Atalante would only marry the suitor who could race after her and catch her whereas here it is the woman who runs after the man; that is she has become the pursuer as opposed to the object of the pursuit. It is no wonder that the Romantic narrator feels threatened.

The narrator's attempt to erase Adélaïde's physical presence is repeated when he recounts hearing her improvise songs with her sister and realizing that she is a gifted musician and poet. He is stunned: "Cette vierge de 18 ans à qui le mot d'amour semblait n'offrir qu'un sens de métaphysique sublime, était plus inspirée que moi/This eigtheen year old virgin for whom the word love seemed only to have a sublime metaphysical meaning was more inspired than I was." (230) His acknowledgement of her superiority is phrased in a way which implies that again she is not a woman. The word "vierge" followed by metaphysics removes her from the sphere of reality and the experience of love.

The figure of Adélaïde is thus used to further discredit the authority of the narrator since both her presence and his representation of her contradict his ideological construction of woman as a projection of man's desire. As she had in *Horace,* Sand works through the patriarchal filter of the male narrator to undermine the very authority of the narrator. What is new in *Valvèdre*, however, is the extent to which the novel presents versions of womanhood that are a direct challenge to the narrator's denial that such beings exist. Moreover, the figure of the woman who suffers because she has internalized Romantic ideals is also presented as a strong character. This type of woman is no longer presented as a sheer victim like Marthe was in *Horace* but as a figure who, although profoundly mistaken, has the potential to change her allegiance to a gender ideology that is destructive for women as well as for men. Sand's life long insistence that women's status would change only through education receives one of its strongest statements here.

Less than two years after *Valvèdre*, Sand published a novel entitled *Mademoiselle la Quintinie* in which she attacked the Catholic church. Her "roman terrible" as her companion Manceau called it (*Corr XVII*: Note 221), was a rebuttal against the pro-catholic serial *Histoire de Sibylle* by Octave Feuillet, which had been published in the *Revue des Deux Mondes* the previous Fall.[7] Feuillet's novel told the story of Sibylle, a pious young aristocratic woman who comes to love and be loved by a worthy, accomplished man who is her perfect match. However, the heroine breaks up with him because he does not believe in God. The novel ends with his sudden conversion and her death. The novel's ideological underpinnings—there is no salvation outside the Catholic church, preferably among aristocrats—, its attack on the spirit of the *siècle* (i.e., lack of moral foundation, widespread doubt, useless science), and its fawning representation of heroic old priests, angel-like duchesses and corrupt commoners, were made to offend Sand who proceded to pen a rebuttal that targeted the hypocrisy, intolerance, and shaky moral grounds of the Church, especially in connection with the celibacy of priests and confession. As her correspondance attests, she was well aware of the dangers of publishing an anti-Catholic novel at a time when the Catholic church seemed all-powerful in France, and she expected to have run-ins with censorship. She did not. The novel was published in its entirety in serial form in the *Revue des Deux Mondes* in Spring of 1863, and in book form later that summer. The book was not censored, although, in December of that year, all of her works were put in the Index by the Church.

Nowadays, however, what strikes us in *Mademoiselle la Quintinie* is not so much Sand's attack on the influence of the Church[8], which she had àlready registered in *Valvèdre*, but the degree to which this influence is seen in terms of gender. When Sand attacks confession, she attacks it as the priest's attempt to influence a wife whose allegiance should be to her husband. Sand summarized her novel to her publisher Buloz in these terms "le voici, ce sujet, Un jeune homme et une jeune fille qui vont se marier, et un confesseur qui veut bien laisser le corps au mari mais qui veut garder l'âme, parce que lui aussi il aime, avec platonisme, avec mysticisme, avec toute la pureté qu'on voudra, mais avec la passion de domination qui caractérise le prêtre. Pour conclure, la jeune fille voit clair et reconnaît qu'entre un mari et une femme, il ne peut y avoir un autre homme/here is the story. A young man and a young woman who are to be married and a confessor who is willing to leave the body to the husband but who wants to keep the soul because he too loves, platonically, mystically, with all the purity one can desire, but with the passion for domination that is characteristic of priests. To sum up, the young woman sees clearly, and recognizes that between husband and wife there cannot be another man." (*Correspondence*, 2 Nov. 62, Vol XVII, 272-73). Sand's attack on the church may have been radical but her view of women as a stake that should be properly claimed by a (Republican and properly enlightened) husband rather than by a priest seems a step back from the gender politics of *Valvèdre*.

Although Sand clearly condemns the priest Moreali's desire for influence and even complete control of the title character Lucie La Quintinie (in fact, he wants her to become a nun and create a convent which he will control), the novel rejects the church's subjection of women only to throw them under the tutelage of patriarchal figures, be they a Romantic figure like Lucie's fiance Emile Lemontier, a conservative like the aspiring writer and friend of Emile, Henri, or even Emile's father, a thinker famous for his anticatholic philosophy. Unlike the narrative situation in *Valvédre*, *Mademoiselle la Quintinie* gives little space to the direct expression of the woman characters. With one exception, the novel is composed of letters written by Emile Lemontier to his father, his father's replies, Henri's letters and the priest Moreali's letters and explanations. Lucie's letters comprise a few short notes to Moreali and a long letter to Emile's father who is presented as the voice of rationality.

The letters written by the male characters rarely express, even indirectly, the point of view of women; even though the letters reproduce in direct discourse a number of Lucie's conversations, they are most often framed and interpreted by the presentation of a male character. Henri, who is engaged to Elise, one of Lucie's convent friends, present views of women and marriage that seem opposed to that of Emile. Because Henri's economic position is precarious (he had a good job but his father has spent the family fortune), he looks at marriage as a business venture that will allow him to stabilize his situation. Moreover, as he confides to Emile, he despises women, "Toutes celles que j'ai connues intimement jouaient un rôle quelconque/All those I have known very well played a role"; he adds "pourvu qu'elle soit de bonne foi dans le caractère qu'elle me montrera, je saurais la choisir, te dis-je, et je l'aiderai à marcher droit, je l'y contraindrai au besoin/as long as she is honest in the personality that she will reveal to me, I will know how to choose her, I tell you, and I shall help her walk straight. If need be, I shall force her to do so." (17). Henri's view of women as inferior beings whose fortune may be the salvation of men but who need to be kept on a short leash is staunchly opposed by Emile who writes to his father about Henri's "lieu commun révoltant, qu'il lui [woman] faut un frein autre que l'amour et le respect de son mari, parce qu'elle n'a pas assez de force morale pour s'en contenter/revolting platitude that she needs a brake other than love and respect for her husband, because she does not have enough moral strength to find it sufficient" (47). Interestingly, Emile's rejection has to do as much with Henri's argument that the Church does provide a check against women's propensity to immorality than with the belief that women are inferior to men. Emile's subsequent discussion with Lucie about the Church's opposition to love between a husband and a wife makes clear that he rejects the Church's influence on women not so much because it keeps women in moral bondage but because it prevents them from properly loving their husbands.

The love that Emile advocates seems a Romantic love superior to Henri's bourgeois kind of "love" but, as we shall see, in both versions, the position that is privileged is the male position (here Sand is counterbalancing Feuillet's conservative views and representation of women as wielding the power). Emile's initial description of his love for Lucie is parallel to that of the narrator in *Valvèdre*. His descriptions of Lucie mostly reveal his sense of powerlessness (both in terms of the effect she has on him and of the role of fate), his jealousy (i.e., his desire to possess her physically and morally), and his lack of understanding. In good Romantic fashion Emile acknowledges the powerful physical effect that Lucie has on him. He writes to his father "mon coeur m'étouffe et ma main tremble rien qu'à écrire son nom/my heart is ready to explode and my hand shakes just from writing her name" (2). When she looks at him in the beginning of their acquaintance, he reacts thus "elle m'a pris mon coeur comme si elle me le tirait de la poitrine avec ses deux mains/she took my heart as if she was pulling it from my chest with her two hands" (4). When he speaks of her voice, he reports being shaken by "secousses électriques/electric shocks" (11) of fascinating power (11). He admits being incapable of actually describing her as "son image remplit le monde et ne saurait être concentrée/her image fills the world and could not be concentrated " (4) and "Ses yeux sont d'une limpidité que je n'ai jamais trouvé dans les yeux noirs. Ils ne sont pas noirs du reste/The limpidity of her eyes is such as I have never seen before in black eyes. They are not black anyway. (12)" Emile's description points back to himself in a narcissistic movement that Sand had explored in *Valvèdre*. His feeling of powerlessness is underlined by his allusion to fate "doit-on être ainsi la proie des antiques fatalités et des instincts aveugles/must one be the prey of ancient fate and blind instincts?" (5) "le hasard ou plutôt ma destinée m'a conduit au château de Turdy [where Lucie resides]/chance or rather my destiny has led me to the Turdy castle" (6). His description with its sense of lack of control and irrational attraction to the feminine figure indicates that the question of Emile's opposition to having his future wife confessed by a priest and influenced by him is a question of power.

Emile must be the sole influence on Lucie and must change her religious beliefs in order to regain the power that his attraction for her has led him to lose, even if he words his position less coarsely. Interestingly, when he responds to his father's advice to fight the influence of the priest over Lucie, the fight is expressed in terms of being a "man." His father describes allowing Emile's wife and children to be devout Catholics as the equivalent of "laisser étouffer en eux le sens *viril* and divin/allow virile and divine sense to be crushed" (70), to which Emile responds "Je veux être un homme/I want to be a man" (71), and later "Tu m'a traité comme un homme/You treated me like a man" (72). Later when lucie asks him to grant her her "liberté de conscience" he refuses saying "je suis un homme et je ne puis supporter un autre homme que moi auprès de vous/I am a man and I cannot bear to have a man other than myself near you." (188). The struggle against the church that was started as the struggle of rationality (represented by Emile and his father) against irrationality and hypocrisy (represented by Moreali) becomes a gender struggle, the struggle to be a man by controlling a woman. Being rational has become being a man, and being a man turns out to mean being able to control a woman; in Emile's case it is controlling the woman who has caused him to feel the loss of his rationality.

Although Emile is not as bourgeois nor as coarse as Henri who confides "Le mari doit être le maître/the husband must be the master" (195) or as Lucie's father, a military man of little sense and sensibility who states "ma fille est ma chose, elle est mon sang, elle m'appartient au même titre que mon bras/my daughter is my thing, my blood. She belongs to me the way my own arm does." (214), Emile's Romantic love and his desire to save Lucy from the clutch of the misguided priest thinly veil his own need for power. After claiming his desire to be a man, he states "*Conquérir* celle que j'aime, la *disputer* à une mortelle figure, la sauver, *l'emmener* avec moi dans la sphère de l'amour vrai, la rendre digne de cette passion sacrée que j'ai pour elle/To conquer the one I love, to contend with a mortal figure for her, to take her with me in the sphere of true love, to make her worthy of the sacred passion that I feel for her." (72). He follows this revealing statement by mentioning the problem he has with attempting to enlighten Lucie's religious beliefs while respecting her freedom, but it is clear that the only freedom he can conceive of is the freedom she has to submit to his guidance. Lucie, who although pious is very intelligent, understands the stakes at play when she pleads "j'ai beau être une femme, encore un enfant à bien des égards, vous savez que chacun tient à sa croyance et que les faibles ont le droit de se défendre contre les forts/I may be a woman, a child still in many respects but you know how important one's beliefs are and you know that the weak have the right to defend themselves against the strong." (31). Lucie articulates the subtext of the novel: because of their weak positions, women are caught between the pernicious influence of the church and the demands for submission of their husbands. Although Sand presents Emile and his father as models of rationality who are legitimately fighting against the abuses of the church, somehow her representation of the gendering of their struggle reveals the ideological underpinnings precisely in terms of gender and the limits of their enlightenment. When she wrote the novel, Sand's avowed intent was to attack the church and her interest quickly shifted to the character and the motivations of the priest[9] but, nonetheless, it is striking that this attack on the church also invokes the limitations of Romanticism for women's autonomy.

Along with these limitations, the novel registers, albeit in a more muted way than in *Valvédre*, the women's internalization of patriarchal notions of their moral and intellectual inferiority. For instance, Lucy refers to her weakness whereas the narrative reveals her resolve and her thoughfulness. Her self-deprecating posture, which reflects Emile's own adoring but patronizing assessment is to be contrasted with the description provided earlier by Mme Marsanne, Elise's mother, who describes Lucie as a "femme réllement supérieure/truly superior woman." To which she adds that "Elle a tant de goût et de bons sens, qu'elle le cache plutôt qu'elle ne le montre; mais il paraît qu'elle est aussi instruite qu'une femme peut l'être...avec cela un caractère qui, par le courage et l'élèvation, ne paraît pas de son sexe/She has so much taste and common sense that she hides it rather than showing it; but it is said that that she is as learned as a woman can ever be...with that a personality that, in terms of courage and high-mindedness, does not seem to belong to her sex." (24-25). The expression "femme supérieure" which had also been used about Adelaïde in *Valvèdre*, denotes a woman who has gone beyond the moral and intellectual limitations imposed on women. However, the rest of Madame Marsanne's comments shows that being a superior woman implies a lack in women in general (for instance, a lack of courage or a lack of sense), and that the qualities that belie the presumed inferiority of women must be hidden, as Lucie does hide them. Last, the comment that Lucie is as educated as a woman can be remind the reader again of the cultural limitations placed on and accepted by most women.

Among the limitations bearing on women's progress, Sand argues here that the biggest one is that placed by the church. The sub-plot involving Lucie's mother, Blanche, focuses Sand's blame on the celibacy of priests and their use of confession to control women. Blanche, who died shortly after the birth of her daughter, was an impressionable young woman who fell under the charm of her young and attractive confessor, Moreali. Of course, she could not admit or quench her love, and, once married to a military man, reverted to a masochistic religious fervor. In a letter to Moreali, Blanche recognizes the self-destructive character of her devotion to the priest "nous [i.e., devout women] n'aimons que ce qui nous dédaigne et nous brise/we only love what scorns and breaks us" (306). And indeed Moreali is shown to despise women (he speaks, among other things, of their lack of logic), and to survive his celibacy by transforming his desire of women into hatred (he follows unknown women who look like Blanche and has fantasies of murder). Descriptions of Moreali make clear that he is not a bad man; simply that as a Catholic priest he is forced to thwart nature and to become a freak[10]. Similarly, Blanche's disgust at her married state, which she terms "une honte et un abrutissement/shameful and debasing" (306) seems to be an indictment of marriage more than a criticsm of the church, but the analysis provided by M. Lemontier when he talks to Moreali shows that her unhappiness and her poor choice of husband is the result of her involvement with the Church: "Il [her devotion and love for her confessor] avait tué le discernement, puisque, par réaction contre les ardeurs secrètes de votre amour sans solution, elle avait choisi l'époux le plus matériel et le moins fait pour la charmer/It had killed judgement since, in reaction against the secret ardors of your love without issue, she had chosen the grossest husband and one least fit to please her." (329). In other words, Lucie's mother lack of discernment is not blamed on her but on the cultural mechanisms through which women are led to make those poor choices.

Sand shows that as a powerful cultural institution, the Church is responsible for the enduring inferior intellectual and emotional status of women, but she also shows that the Romantic ideology that opposed the conservative power of the church is also part of a patriarchal structure that limits women. Even in a polemical novel like *Mademoiselle la Quintinie* where Sand uses a Romantic character like Emile Lemontier to voice her opposition to the Church, Sand cannot help but undermine Romantic narrative authority and values as she had done in previous novels. She demonstrates the complexity of ideological positions when gender is part of the equation. Even though she shows that at the political or cultural level, a position like Emile's position (for instance, his desire for a loving relationship with his wife rather than the bourgeois material arrangement of his friend Henri) is superior to the oppression of the church, she also suggests that in terms of gender, this enlightened position may still be oppressive, or at least patronizing. Last she shows how women can be led to participate in their own victimization.

NOTES

1. He notes that out of some seventy novels, only three use a female narrative voice.

2. Although little is known about the composition of the novel, the material conditions of its publication are known and indicative of the political stakes it raised. Sand started *Horace* in 1841 and called it *L'étudiant*, title which indicates her awareness of her characters'status as types. The avowed purpose of the novel was to describe that enlightened section of the bourgeoisie which had been maligned by the journalist Gigault de la Bédollière in his recently published *L'étudiant en droit*. However, this declared goal was soon superseded by the more radical one of describing marginals (i.e., workers and women) and the mechanisms of their exploitation by the educated bourgeoisie. Before *Horace* was finished, Sand had received a substantial cash advance from her editor Buloz for publication in installments in the *Revue des Deux Mondes*. However, Buloz requested changes to tone down the manuscript. The laws of September 1835 which muzzled the press were still in effect and he feared to be indicted under one of the numerous "délit d'opinion de presse " which included "any attacks against the principle or the form of the regime established in 1830" (*Histoire générale de la presse française* 113). Sand did not appreciate being asked to censor herself especially since at that time she was engaged in a law suit against Buloz concerning copyrights; but she had signed a contract and spent a good part of her advance. She consulted the socialist Pierre Leroux who helped her break her contract and proposed to create *La Revue Indépendante*, a socialist organ in which *Horace* would be published. As Samuel Bernstein notes in his *Auguste Blanqui and the Art of Insurrection*, *Horace* was thus the impetus for the creation of an influential socialist publication which was to benefit from Sand's large reading public. The publication context for *Horace* reflects the complexity of Sand's strategies for describing the silencing of women and of workers.

3. According to Sand's correspondance, at the time Maurice Sand was working on a book on butterflies *Le Monde des Papillons*, which was to be published in 1867 (*Corr* XVI: 835). He also produced a geological study of feldspaths (*Corr* XVI: 841). George Sand considerably edited and corrected both works.

4. Sand's description of birthgiving and motherhood as involving specific bodies of knowledge which can be claimed by women reminds us, as Roddy Reid states in *Families in Jeopardy: Regulating the Social Body in France*, that the nineteenth-century saw the exclusion of women from the medical field by male doctors who took over obstetrics, a field

where women had traditionally excelled. Valvèdre's statement about the science of motherhood can be seen as a further example of the male invasion of obstetrics and pediatrics, except that he turns over this science to another woman, his sister.

5. The initial description of Moserwald by the narrator is full of nineteenth-century antisemitic clichés; however, his narrative position at the end of the novel as a close friend of the positive protagonists deflects these clichés.

6. Actually the 1860's and 1870's saw an exacerbation of Republican anticlericalism, which Sand shared and which led to her publication of *Mademoiselle la Quintinie* (1863). A few years later, the main theme of the Republican campaign for the legislative elections was the threat of the church to individuals and family, especially through the confession of women (See Pierre Albertini, *La France du 19 siècle* for a description of the growth of anticlericalism).

7. The first part was published August 15, 1862 (777-841), the second part September 1 (39-84), the third part September 15 (241-70), and the last part October 1 (552-609).

8. Robert Godwin-Jones, who is one of the few recent critics to talk about *Mademoiselle la Quintinie*, is surprised by Sand's "aggressiveness" and "intolerance" against Catholicism (Godwin-Jones 270) but her novel is a response against Feuillet's attack on the values that Sand cherishes.

9. The correspondance reveals her awareness of Lucie's increasing passivity as she called it "Melle la Quintinie devient nécessairement un peu passive vers la fin, et Moreali absorbe tout/necessarily becomes somewhat passive near the end, and Moreali takes up everything" (*Correspondence* XVII, letter to Buloz, 07/02/63, p. 438). Sand also wanted to change her title to "Le roman d'un prêtre/The story of a priest."

10. The contrast between Moreali and Feuillet's Abbé Renaud is striking. Renaud is quite old, mild, mediocre, and totally sexless. Actually, at the beginning of the novel he is so uninspiring that Sibylle's faith is shaken.

CHAPTER IV
THE MAN WITHIN OR THE LIMITS
OF ANDROGYNY:
GABRIEL AND *LUCREZIA FLORIANI*

Throughout her fiction George Sand not only destabilized Romantic narrative authority, as we have seen in the preceding chapter, but also repeatedly explored the question of the construction of gender identity and challenged contemporary representations of the feminine. *Gabriel* (1840) and *Lucrezia Floriani* (1846) in particular offer striking examples of the ways in which she represented constructed gender identity and the price paid by women for having internalized patriarchal cultural models. *Gabriel* questions gender identity through an exploration of the complexity of cross-dressing as a means to disrupt the patriarchal order; while *Lucrezia Floriani* focuses on the paradoxically empowering and victimizing effect that the adoption of a maternal model has on independent women. Although these novels are not well-known, even by Sand's scholars, they deserve much attention especially as scholarly discourse is paying increasing attention to the ways women were able to start representing themselves. Since nineteenth-century fiction was one major area of discourse in which women participated in great numbers as writers and as readers, we need to look closely at the works where this self-representation occurs. Sand, who was usually very casual about her works (she even sometimes said she could not remember having written certain things), paid particular attention to the writing and the dissemination of these two works. For instance, as her correspondance attests[1] she went to great efforts to have *Gabriel* performed, and she totally rewrote *Lucrezia Floriani* even though her manuscript was finished when she left Paris for Nohant in Spring 1846 and even though she had a contract. Her unusual concern for these works' reception may indicate that she was aware of the significance of these novels.

 Gabriel's exploration of cross-dressing must be read in light of the recent critical inquiry that has theorized cross-dressing "as an incursion into the territory that crosses gender boundaries (viii Bullough) but without mentioning works like *Gabriel*. In *Vested Interests, Cross-Dressing and Cultural Anxiety*, Marjorie Garber has argued that cross-dressing introduces a cultural crisis by challenging "easy notions of binarity, putting into question the categories of 'female' and 'male,' whether they are considered essential or constructed, biological or essential." (10). For Garber, the very fact of cross-dressing constitutes a crisis in established cultural structures based on binary opposites but Julia Esptein and Kristina Straub in *Body Guards: The Cultural Politics of Gender Ambiguity* have pointed out the "problematic nature of gender ambiguity as resistance to patriarchal structures." In other words, cross-dressing can both disrupt and reinforce binary opposites. Indeed, in her study of eighteenth-century fiction by women, Catherine Craft-Fairchild has showed that although theorized as sexually enabling, transvestism or role-reversal is insufficient to challenge patriarchal hierarchies or "oppressive binary logic" (172). Craft-Fairchild further shows that in the British women writers she has studied, masquerade (i.e., cross-dressing as a male) appears "as a disempowering capitulation to patriarchal structures that posit female subordination." (172).

Similarly, in her critique of Michel Foucault's edition of the nineteenth-century hermaphrodite/cross-dresser Herculine Barbin (born 1838), Judith Butler points out that, far from expressing some primary sexual multiplicity as Foucault would have it, Herculine's gender ambiguity is anything but a transgression of the law; on the contrary "s/he embodies the law, not as an entitled subject but as an enacted testimony to the law's uncanny capacity to produce only those rebellions that it can guarantee will—out of fidelity—defeat themselves and those subjects who, utterly subjected, have no choice but to reiterate the law of their genesis" (*Gender Trouble* 106). But Sand's *Gabriel* is altogether different: Sand's story is not simply a representation of the constructedness of gender identity and of the inevitability of Gabriel's subjection. Although the novel/play starts with an articulation of cross-dressing as a manifestation of the power of the paternal law, it evolves from within the law into a subversion of its terms.

The character Gabriel (biologically female, but brought up as a male) will be referred to as "s/he." Sand's own practice in the list of characters and in the stage directions throughout the play was to use "he" for obvious reasons of suspense. The faithful servant Marc also always addresses Gabriel in the masculine form (with, significantly, one exception after Gabriel has been murdered). Mark's position in the power structure of the novel is as problematic as that of Gabriel and he ends up being the only male character whose existence doesn't depend on the appropriation or extinction of Gabriel's identity. The use of "s/he" by its very indeterminacy is also a reminder of the artificiality and inadequacy of binary terms to describe sexual and gender differences: as Sand demonstrates, Gabriel is more or less than he or she, but her body is literally and symbolically the location of the split.

Moreover, the hybrid form of the work, neither a novel nor a play, contributes to the blurring of categories which is the theme of the work while giving the readers direct access to the voice of Gabriel. This lack of mediation is to be put in contrast with the example of Herculine Barbin's story mentioned earlier: a story framed by the powerful interpretive discourse of Michel Foucault and by the fictionalized version "A Scandal at the Convent" authored by Oscar Panizza. The only mediation in *Gabriel* is the half page foreword in which George Sand describes the context in which she wrote *Gabriel* "mes enfants jouant autour de moi dans une chambre d'auberge/my children playing around me in my hotel room" (43); a reassuring foreword about a woman author with a man's name who can both wield the pen and care for her children as she is writing about a human being whose sex is the site of a cultural battle[2].

In *Gabriel*, cross-dressing is first represented as a patriarchal injunction and as a prohibition of desire. At the beginning of the novel/play, we learn that, following the order of his grandfather, Gabriel has been brought up in isolation as a male in order to keep the family assets and title in the senior line of descent. According to Salic law, as a female heir, Gabriel could not inherit the family fortune, which would then revert to Astophe the male heir of the younger branch. Gabriel has been brought up by a priest and a servant Marc who are the only ones to know the secret and, at the beginning of the play, the old Bramante prince has come to tell Gabriel that s/he is not a male but that s/he must continue to cross-dress for the sake of the family reputation. As his priest-tutor explains, Gabriel's education has emphasized the "la grandeur du rôle masculin/the greatness of the masculine role" and the "l'abjection du rôle féminin dans la nature et dans la société/abjection of the feminine role in nature and society"[3] (53) so that there is no doubt that Gabriel will agree to choose "freedom and power" (i.e., pretend to be male) over "weakness and slavery," as the priest and Bramante are referring to life as a woman.

This first scene is striking in the heavy use of the vocabulary of law[4] and coercion and in the organization of class, gender, and genealogical or racial distinctions around the axis of power; we are presented with a series of binary opposites: master/servant; man/woman; oldest heir/youngest heir in which a given individual may switch position from one category to another but for the sake of preserving the hierarchical binary structure. Thus Bramante has engineered the cross-dressing of Gabriel (an apparent blurring of gender lines) in order to strengthen the purity of his descent (that is of a hierarchical conception of "race[5]"). In the discussion about Gabriel's upbringing, the tutor refers to masculine and feminine in terms of "roles" (52), thus reinforcing the notion that sex and gender are a structure composed of binary elements whose contents depend on the overall hierarchy. Here genealogy (or "race") takes precedence over gender exclusion.[6] Bramante makes clear Gabriel's options "entre le sort brillant d'un prince et l'éternelle captivité du cloître, choisissez/between the brilliant lot of a prince and the eternal captivity of a cloister, choose." (70). Clearly cross-dressing here is a submission to this paternal injunction, but it is a double submission: a submission to an external coercion and an internalization of the patriarchal law. Indeed, Gabriel sees the lie about his biological sex as a "un vol que les lois puniraient avec la dernière ignominie/theft that laws would punish with the utmost shame" (70); that is s/he accepts the general law which assigns fortunes according to the sex of the heir, empowering male descendants over female ones. Gabriel thus plans to live as a man in order to restore the family fortune to his male cousin.

        The second striking characteristic of the initial context of Gabriel's cross-dressing is the representation of the prohibition of desire. After been told that s/he is not a male, Gabriel threatens his grandfather with taking his life to thwart his plans (70). The Prince's answer reveals another stake of cross-dressing "la concupiscence parle-t-elle déjà tellement à vos sens que l'idée d'une éternelle chasteté vous exaspère à ce point/Does lust already speak so much to your senses that the idea of eternal chastity aggravates you so?" Although his comment is meant to be merely insulting, the Prince articulates what Gabriel will lose as a woman cross-dressing: i.e., the ability to express sexual desire. Ironically the "eternal chastity" as Bramante calls it, to which Gabriel is bound if he accepts to live as a man is also the fate that awaits him if s/he lives as a woman since s/he is threatened with the "eternal captivity of the convent" (70). In other words, cross-dressing is here represented as an instrumental strategy through which an individual who is biologically female can experience the freedom of a man within the parameters of patriarchal law, but cannot live her desire. At this level, Gabriel's cross-dressing does not appear to be symptomatic of any category crisis as Garber has argued in general. Rather, it reinscribes the hierarchy of the sexes and the prohibition against women's pleasure. Sand's fictional representation of cross-dressing confirms the findings of Bullough and Bullough's *Cross-dressing, Sex, and Gender* in which they report that a high number of women have cross-dressed throughout history in order to avoid the restriction put on the female sex. However, they point out that, although these women lived as men, they avoided being found out by restraining from having heterosexual relationships with their partners. Although Garber finds the "appropriation of transvestism in the service of a humanist 'progress narrative" (i.e., women living as men because they will have more freedom and success) problematic (Garber 70), and although she would like to read cross-dressing as a space of "erotic pleasure and play" (70), Gabriel's situation and the cases reported by Bullough suggest that this "play space" is reserved for cross-dressers who are men.[7]

Thus, paradoxically, if cross-dressing blurs gender boundaries, it also operates at the service of the patriarchal law that limits female sexuality to reproduction, or in the extreme version of patriarchal law represented by the Prince Bramante, female desire is simply prohibited.[8] When Bramante asks the tutor whether Gabriel does suspect the truth (i.e., that s/he is a "woman"), the tutor reassures him that Gabriel's education has been "so chaste" and his thoughts "so pure" (54) that Gabriel is convinced he is a man as he was told. Although at the realistic level this seems hard to believe, their conviction, or more accurately, their fantasy that Gabriel, as a biological female brought up as male, is totally ignorant of anatomical differences between the sexes, this fantasy is perfectly in keeping with the patriarchal prohibition against woman's desire and woman's knowledge.

Actually the assumption that being a woman is to occupy the position of the subject not-supposed to know is so widespread that readers have often failed to realize the significance of Gabriel's monologue in scene vi where s/he reveals that s/he does know "this horrible secret" (72), as s/he calls it. S/he adds "Les insensés! Comment pouvaient-ils croire que j'étais encore la dupe de leur insolent artifice/How mad they are! How could they believe that I was still duped by their insolent artifice!" (72).

The beginning scenes of the play thus need to be reread in light of Gabriel's self-knowledge. The scene where s/he recounts her dream of being a winged maiden "vêtue d'une longue robe flottante/garbed in a long flowing dress" (60) to the tutor, rejecting his interpretation that in the dream Gabriel was an angel (i.e., a sexless creature) must be read, not as Gabriel's "intuition" of her essential nature[9], but as Gabriel's articulation of self-knowledge, and as his claiming a sexed nature, albeit not within the traditional binary terms. The dream is Gabriel's dream and s/he knows how to interpret it, an interesting deviation from the expected psychoanalytic model where the female patient's lack of knowledge is gradually remedied by a male authority.

But what does Gabriel know? That s/he has some female anatomical characteristics, that educated as a male s/he has enjoyed the freedom of the cultural dominant element but that s/he feels neither male nor female. S/he says "je ne sens pas que mon âme ait un sexe/I don't feel that my being has a sex" (57). That is, Gabriel rejects the culturally hierarchical binary system that regulates gender and sexual differences; and s/he embodies, to borrow from the Cuban cross-dresser writer Severo Sardui "the coexistence of masculine and feminine signifiers in a single body" (*Written on a Body* 37), a dangerous mix that will threaten the stability of sexual, hierarchical, and conceptual boundaries; and of course that will be evicted. This eviction, as we shall see, will not be a simple vanishing, but a violent murder which will implicate all the individuals who represent the patriarchal law and which will position the readers on the side of the victim, i.e., of a body in which binary sexual and gender differences are blurred.

As we have seen, Gabriel's cross-dressing occurs within the patriarchal law represented by Bramante's manipulation, by Gabriel's own internalization of that law, but it is also a blurring of sexual differences. This blurring (a woman dressing as a man who has both feminine and masculine characteristics) proves to be very attractive to the male characters that Gabriel meets, especially to his cousin Astophe. Gabriel's cross-dressing will threaten those characters's status as males by triggering unackowledged homosexual longings. Gabriel seeks out Astophe in a tavern and they both end up in jail after murdering in self-defense two men who attacked them. While the attractive, debauchee, and impoverished Astophe[10] sleeps off his wine and the murders, Gabriel ponders the nature of courage and his meeting with his cousin under such violent circumstances.

By accepting the patriarchal law that favors male heirs and by wanting to give her cousin his money, Gabriel has symbolically murdered the woman in her. Astophe, who uses and abuses his prerogatives as a male, is powerfully attracted to Gabriel and troubled by the fact that Gabriel possesses physical feminine and masculine traits. The more attraction Astophe feels for Gabriel, the more he comments on women's inferiority or mistreats his mistress, the courtesan Faustina. In other words, his sense of masculinity is somewhat restored by his abuse of femininity.

Finally, in order to face his homosexual desire for Gabriel (who, although a female, functions as a male) and feeling threatened in his status as a male, Astophe asks Gabriel to go to a party during carnival dressed as a woman. Sand obviously knew the function of carnival as an occasion for cross-dressing, for class and sexual transgression: Astophe says to Gabriel "Chacun revêt l'effigie de ce qu'il désire être ou désire posséder: le valet s'habille en maître, l'imbécile en docteur; moi je t'habille en femme/Each adopts the effigy of what he wants to be or wants to have: the servant dresses as a master, the idiot as a doctor; and I dress you as a woman" (111). Astophe wants Gabriel to be a woman so that he can be a "man."

He can only face his desire for Gabriel if Gabriel plays the role of a woman, i.e., of an object that can be owned. Here again cross-dressing is represented as the space where transgressions occur but the transgression in question is complex. First, it operates a blurring of sexual boundaries: from heterosexual to homosexual; two, it reinscribes patriarchal gender boundaries: dressing as a woman means that Gabriel will become the object of Astophe's masculine desire to possess; three, it is a transgression against the patriarchal law prohibiting woman's desire. Gabriel revealingly acknowledges "je n'ai pu résister au désir imprudent de faire cette experience! Quel effet vais-je produire sur lui/I couldn't resist the imprudent desire to try this out. What effect will I have on him?" (108). Gabriel's willingness to "back cross-dress" so to speak is couched in terms of her own desire: sexual desire for Astophe and desire for knowledge: what will happen when the part of him that is woman is allowed to emerge?

Gabriel's experiment in the breakdown of sexual boundaries creates havoc: at the party, the men pursue him/her, the women and Astophe are jealous. When the men are finally told the "truth" (that Gabriel is a "man," they are quite disturbed: the revelation of what they think is their desire for another man is so threatening that one of them, Antonio, will later provoke Gabriel in a duel during which he will be wounded, both physically and symbolically in his masculinity, finally convinced that Gabriel can only be a man.

If Gabriel's cross-dressing and back cross-dressing reveal the instability of masculine heterosexuality, it also reveals Gabriel's own desire. After leaving the party and being kissed by her cousin, Gabriel undresses violently with these words "retrouverais-je sous mon pourpoint le calme de mon sang et l'innocence de mes pensées/Shall I be able to recover under my doublet the cool of my blood and my innocent thoughts?" (126)... "Sa dernière étreinte me dévorait/his last embrace consumed me." Almost immediately after Gabriel articulates her sexual desire, Astophe discovers him bare-chested and identifies him as a woman, that is as the justification of his own desire. The rest of Sand's play uncovers the price paid by Gabriel's acknowledgment of her desire as a woman in a world regulated by masculinist ideologies; and describes the mechanisms through which an ambiguous body and mind is outlawed.

Once Gabriel is found out by Astophe and once s/he accepts to live as a woman with him, Astophe becomes tyrannical and jealous in a movement which Sand will repeat and amplify in *Lucrezia Floriani*. Although Gabriel lives as a woman part of the year in an isolated house in the countryside, Astophe becomes increasingly jealous of the time when Gabriel cross-dresses as a man and lives in town because Astophe fears Gabriel's closeness with other men. In other words, Astophe can only love Gabriel as a woman in bondage. Interestingly enough, Gabriel, who is marked by masculine and feminine signifiers, is in complete isolation. The only women characters presented are stereotypical "negative elaboration of the masculine subject" to borrow Irigaray's expression (Butler 103).[11] The presence of such negative elaborations emphasize the problematic nature of a notion of "woman" or "femininity" constructed from a patriarchal hierarchy. One such woman image is the courtesan Faustina who has no autonomy and whose body and soul are for sale. The other is Astophe's mother Septtima whose whole existence focuses on her role as Astophe's jealous mother/servant and on her hate for Gabriel who, living as a woman under her roof, challenges Septtima's patriarchal notion of women as servants without physical, intellectual, and moral freedom. The third one is Astophe's religious aunt Barbe whose name is humorously symbolic: of course a beard is a conventional sign for masculinity—Barbe represents "woman" as a negative construction; and Barbe was the name of a Christian martyr who was decapitated by her father, a telling comment on the price paid by women for submitting to the law of the father. Interestingly also, Gabriel, even when she lives as a woman, never gets pregnant even though she has a long affair with Astophe. She thus disrupts nineteenth-century ideology according to which women's sexuality is subsumed to reproduction.[12]

Thus in *Gabriel* there are no women, and we might add there are no men. There are only gendered individuals conforming to binary divisions set up to reinforce power structures. The power and the threat of Gabriel is that as a cross-dresser s/he calls attention to the arbitrariness of binary distinctions between male/female, masculine/feminine, heterosexual/homosexual by blurring the distinctions between the two even if the occasion for the cross-dressing and its outcome spring from an injunction of the paternal law. Gabriel may die because Bramante has him murdered and because s/he would not abandon his life as a man to please his lover Astophe, but in the process the instability of the category of sexual differences and gender has been uncovered, and the presence and the violence of the patriarchal law has been revealed. It is no wonder that Sand did not succeed in having *Gabriel* performed in the 1840's: such a powerful statement about the links between power, sexuality and gender, and about the violence with which a patriarchal system punishes transgressors was bound to disturb Sand's audience, even as she delivered her message under the seemingly innocuous guise of an attentive mother-author.

The violence of the patriarchal law against women is also the theme of *Lucrezia Floriani* in which Sand depicts another woman who has transgressed the limits of gender boundaries, and whose acceptance of specific cultural norms leads to her demise. Sand published *Lucrezia Floriani* in 1846; she had started the novel in Paris where she lived with her companion Chopin, but she completely revised it when she returned to her country house in Nohant by herself in the month of May. People familiar with the author and her circle created a *succès de scandale* by reading the novel as a *roman à clef*; they claimed they recognized Chopin in the unflattering portrait of the male protagonist, Prince Karol, a Romantic figure whose weakness, intolerance, and jealousy Sand described so precisely.

It is true that at the time Sand was writing the novel, her long liaison with Chopin was slowly coming to an end and they separated the following year. However, Sand staunchly defended herself from having being autobiographical and from having settled scores on paper. Although there are plenty of details that can be linked to Chopin's personality and to the vicissitudes of their liaison[13], what is instructive is how Sand, consciously or not, transformed her experience to produce a work that, very much like *Gabriel*, destabilizes binary gender divisions, valorizes and redefines the feminine, dissects the ideology underpinning the topos of the Romantic hero and Romantic love, and finally demonstrates the destructive effect of her heroine's internalization of such Romantic notions.

The novel starts with a presentation of the male protagonist Prince Karol, a young, melancholy, fastidious aristocrat who is befriended by an energetic young Italian aristocrat, Salvator, who nurtures him especially after the death of his fiancée and of his mother. After six chapters, the narrator introduces Lucrezia Floriani, a friend of Salvador who has retired to the countryside with her children after a glamourous and successful career as an actress and author, to whose estate the two young men arrive by "chance." The plot essentially revolves around Prince Karol's infatuation with Lucrezia and her progressive yielding to his passion. Their long affair (eight years) ends with her slow death caused by the unrelenting jealousy of Prince Karol. There is little suspense as the narrator announces ahead of time what will happen. The preface warns the reader that the novel will not cater to the current gothic tastes (murders, betrayals, etc) of the public but will depict a passion and make the reader think (684). The expressed didactic purpose of the author and the narrator's flippant comments toward plot development point to the fact that the novel is more a general demonstration than a description of specific individuals.

Although Lucrezia is the title character, she appears only after the male protagonists have been presented. She is inscribed into a system of signification that challenges binary oppositions and, at the same time, that emphasizes the presence of a patriarchal world into which the heroine lives. The details used in the portrait of Karol are part of the Romantic topos: he is young, melancholy, extremely attractive and refined. He is presented as not fitting stereotypes of masculinity but at the same time he is not effeminate. The comparisons used in the description suggests a blurring of boundaries involving the masculine and the feminine, the human and the surhuman. His appearance is so exceptional that he has "ni âge ni sexe/neither sex nor age" (689-90). He is compared to an "ange, beau de visage, comme une grande femme triste, pur et svelte de forme comme un jeune dieu de l'Olympe/angel, with a beautiful face, like a tall sad woman, pure and svelte in shape like a young god from Olympus" (689), but "Ce n'était point non plus la gentillesse éfféminée d'un chérubin/it was not the effeminate kindness of a cherub." He has a weak constitution, which makes him interesting to women, and he is "faible et paresseux dans les exercices du corps/weak and lazy in exercises of the body" (692); far from avoiding him, other men sometimes stop their physical activities to keep him company. Karol's very physical weakness is thus a source of seduction for men and women.

Apart from Karol's ambiguously gendered physical appearance, the narrator points out his inability to understand or tolerate difference, and ties it to his relation with his mother: "Il ne comprenait que ce qui était identique à lui-même, sa mère, dont il était un reflet pur et brillant/He only understood what was like himself, his mother, of whom he was a pure and brilliant reflection" (690). Karol was brought up by his mother, a pious, intransigent aristocrat who protected her son from encounters with the rougher aspects of life. Her loss sends Karol into a depression from which Salvador is trying to rescue him. The prince's refined tastes and judgmental attitude made him lose interest in his friends, except, strangely enough, for Salvador, a young man sightly older than he, full of life, who is very devoted to him.[14] Salvador's devotion is explained by Karol's exceptional personality but also by Karol's need for him: "Salvador aimait Karol pour le besoin que ce dernier avait de lui/ loved Karol for the need that Karol had of him" (692). Later on, Salvador's nurturing instincts are mentioned again. The readers are told that Salvador takes care of Karol "like a child" when Karol is sick, although he thinks that Karol is more nervous and impressionable than really sick (692). Karol's nervousness, his physical weakness, his irrational fears, his beauty as well as his dependence on motherly figures who indulge him, be it his actual mother or Salvador, traits that are described directly by the narrator (and thus given authority) make him a figure who hardly fits traditional definitions of masculinity or even "maleness." Similarly, Salvador's interest in nurturing is not typical of masculine figures. Without being "feminine," both male characters share features which upset strict gender boundaries. These characters embody a range of attitudes and behavior that challenges strict separations between the realm of the feminine and the masculine. Salvador, who appears more "masculine' than Karol (he is physically strong, very active physically and sexually), is also a "feminine" nurturing figure. Whereas Salvador's past is not revealed by the narrator, explanations of Karol's upbringing make clear that his personality (i.e., also his gender) is the result of specific circumstances, (his class and his mother's influence), that his identity as a Romantic hero is constructed, the way Gabriel's identity was constructed as a masculine identity.

In contrast to the description of the male protagonist, the presentation of the title character Lucrezia Floriani bypasses the usual emphasis on physical appearance (i.e., on the reaction of a male narrator to the female body). She is introduced by comments uttered by Salvador and by an inn keeper, a minor character. Salvador enthusiastically describes her moral and intellectual qualities (700). When Karol expresses his distaste to be taken to the house of a woman of 'ill-repute" (701) and when he implies that she has been Salvador's mistress, Salvador rebukes him by stating that Lucrezia, who had a lover at the time Salvador knew her, is loyal and faithful and therefore Salvador "never thought to desire her" (701). In other words he links his lack of desire to her moral qualities and to her unavailability. These preliminary judgements by the male characters are followed by the narrator's presentation, which is as positive as that of Salvador, and which focuses on Lucrezia's professional achievements. She was not only a gifted and successful actress but an independent author and producer of plays. The narrator specifies that she left her career at the height of her success and beauty. Lucrezia's financial success is linked to her work, not to her association to powerful lovers or friends (703), a situation, we should note, which is in stark contrast to that of the male characters who have no "work." This presentation challenges the readers' expectations for female characters whose traditional venues for success involve an association with powerful males, be it through inheritance, marriage, or affairs.

Lucrezia's independence and creativity thus contrast with the male characters' idleness—they are rich aristocrats who haven't seriously pursued any activity— and with their dependance on their family wealth to live. Sand uses class differences to challenge cultural expectation of gender differences. Her heroine's gifts are not linked to her body (her beauty or her ability to attract men's desires) but to her intellectual, creative, and moral qualities. In other words, she lives outside the system of patriarchal values.

Sand pushes to the limits of vraisemblance when she also gives Lucrezia an active emotional and sexual life (usually a female character who transgresses social norms is deprived of a rich personal life and is hardly ever allowed to have affairs and to be a good mother). Lucrezia has had several lovers but, as she explains "Les sens ne m'ont jamais emportée avant le coeur/I was never led by my senses before my heart" (703). Although she did not marry, her relations with men were based on genuine love, not on sexual instincts separated from emotional needs. She even claims "devant Dieu être une femme vertueuse/before God to be a virtuous woman" (703). This extremely positive portrait of Lucrezia allows Sand to question the stereotyping of women as angels, i.e., chaste creatures whose experiences take place with society's sanctioned institutions like marriage, or as demons, i.e., unbridled, sex crazed figures of hysteria. Lucrezia is obviously neither. Sand claims for her heroine a range of experiences usually reserved for male protagonists.

Sand's portrait emphasizes Lucrezia's ability to join the realms of the sexual, the emotional, and the familial. Lucrezia is sincerely in love when she has an affair and she believes that it will last. Sand's approval of her character's claim to virtue is clearly marked by her choice of Lucrezia as a first name since it clearly recalls "Lucrèce," the name of the Roman heroine who committed suicide after being raped by Sextus Tarquin[15] and the title of the popular play by François Ponsard (1843). For Sand, however, virtue does not mean violation of the female body followed by death, but integration of the female body into emotional life and survival. Sand redefines women's virtue in a radical way since, rather than focusing on feminine lack of sexual activity as a sign of purity, she emphasizes the virtue of integrating the sexual and the emotional. Unlike male authors of the nineteenth-century who punish their female protagonists for their transgressions (novels by Chateaubriand, Constant, Balzac, Flaubert come to mind), Sand valorizes her heroine and pushes the limits of her transgression, by making her into an exemplary mother whose four children were born of different fathers. Of course, Sand's decision to give different fathers to Lucrezia's children challenges the basis of the patriarchal system. There can only be a paternal line of descent if the mother is monogamous. Maternity is thus presented as a way to undermine paternity claims. If, as Marilyn Lukacher has argued in *Maternal Fictions*, Sand had been preoccupied with the problem of illegitimacy all of her life and if this preoccupation was tied to her anxiety about her origin (represented by the two opposing maternal powers in her life: her aristocratic grandmother and her plebeian mother), by the time she wrote *Lucrezia Floriani*, Sand's interest in illegitimacy had switched from the point of view of the child to that of the mother. Lucrezia Floriani's illegitimate children and her qualities as a mother serve to destabilize the symbolic power of the paternal and emphasize the primacy of the maternal, while allowing Sand to disengage the maternal from the domestic realm, to explore the tensions between the sexual and the maternal, and to examine the consequences of extending maternal power to sexual and emotional relations.

Throughout the novel, the narrator emphasizes Lucrezia's role as an extremely competent and warm mother whose professional activities did not prevent her from being an attentive mother[16]. The reader is told that while Lucrezia was an actress, she would nurse her young children even during performances. The narrator also explains her retreat to the countryside as a desire to protect her children from being ostracized because of her reputation.[17] When one of her children deeply cuts his finger, she very calmly reassures him and takes care of the cut, an incident which Karol finds offensive.

The portrait of Lucrezia, before she is even presented directly to the reader is that of a strong, gifted, successful woman, lover, and mother, who enjoys an unusual degree of control and independence. It is only after the presentation of her intellectual, creative, and moral qualities that the reader is provided with a description of her physical appearance, first through a brief description of Karol's impression, then of Salvador.

By filtering the physical description through two male narrators, Sand indirectly points out the inevitability and the insufficiency of the male gaze. The previous preparatory descriptions of Lucrezia as a moral and creative being appear as a way to correct and to counterbalance the power of the male gaze. Symbolically the men meet her at night when they cannot really see her face. Prince Karol's impression is a negative one. Lucrezia does not look like what he expected of a performer of aristocratic roles: she is not elegant; she is short and plump with a loud voice which grates on his ears (712). Karol's reactions are revealing: Lucrezia is perceived in terms of whether she fits his expectations. The focus has shifted from her to his subjectivity in a way that suggests that power is an integral part of his perception. Similarly, Salvador's reactions register the fact that Lucrezia's appearance is not what he remembered (she has gained weight, has less color, is less lively) from which he concludes that "Elle n'aimait plus: c'était une autre femme/ she no longer loved, she was another woman" (713). He links her diminished glamour and lack of attractiveness (for him, at least) to her lack of sentimental involvement. For Salvador, Lucrezia is her whole self only when she is involved with a man. These two descriptions, which are separated by a description of Lucrezia's house and by the narrator's comments about Lucrezia's benefactress and godmother Lucrezia Ranieri, indicate a similarity of points of view between the two men, a similarity along gender lines, that places Lucrezia as the feminine object of their male critical gaze. Lucrezia Floriani is quite aware of Salvador's reaction and she reacts frankly by remarking on the changes that have affected them both. She contrasts the changes that she sees in him—positive changes; he is now a mature, attractive man—to her getting older. Her comments suggests that Lucrezia's professional and personal strength extends to her reclaiming the gaze. She is aware that Salvador's perception centers around whether or not she is an object of male desire and she correctly assigns it to aging.

Salvador does not understand the meaning of Lucrezia's remark and to soften what he thinks was a "cruel gaze" (714), he follows with comments on her ability to attract lovers even when she is very old. Lucrezia turns his flattery into an occasion to desconstruct feminine beauty and age. She links the ability to remain beautiful and to slow down the effects of aging to idleness and lack of feeling. In other words, the male characters' focus on women's beauty precludes that women work or have an intense emotional life. Lucrezia's comments suggest her awareness of the cost to women and of the class implications of the traditional emphasis on beauty; her comments also serve as a guide to reinterpret the earlier description of Karol's beauty, which must now be read as a sign of his youth and of his belonging to an idle class. [18]

Sand further redefines beauty, not as a male construction based on women's lack of activity and engagement with the world, but as the outward manifestation of energy and harmony. The longest physical description of Lucrezia occurs when, at the end of the evening during which Lucrezia has entertained her two male guests, her children are kissing her goodnight:

> Avec son profil de camée antique, ses cheveux roulés sans art et sans coquetterie autour de sa tête puissante...sa pâleur calme, marbrée par les baisers violents des marmots, ses yeux fatigués,

mais sereins, ses beaux bras, dont les muscles ronds et fermes se dessinaient gracieusement lorsqu'elle y enfermait toute sa couvée, elle devint tout à coup plus belle et plus vivante que Salvador ne l'avait encore vue/With her profile resembling that of an antique cameo, her hair artlessly and unaffectedly coiled around her powerful head...her calm pallor flushed by the violent kisses of her children, her tired but serene eyes, her beautiful arms whose round and firm muscles were gracefully outlined when she encircled the whole of her brood, she suddenly became more beautiful and more alive that Salvador had yet even seen her (717).

The description emphasizes her modesty, her strength, her activity, and her timeless beauty. It is a definition of beauty that bypasses the economy of male desire in that, in the descriptive scheme, the woman described is not a passive element, but an active agent whose activity triggers the description and creates the impression of beauty. Sand's description makes clear that female beauty is not a state, but a constructed perception that is traditionally steeped in a patriarchal signifying system. Later on in the narrative when Prince Karol falls in love with Lucrezia, his reaction is to find a resemblance between her and his mother, in a move which repeats Sand's earlier suggestion that the perception of beauty in women is linked to the mental expectation of the male gazer.

Sand's redefinition of beauty is also accompanied by a redefinition of love, which is articulated as Lucrezia recounts her past relationships and their failure. Lucrezia sees love as a kind of "enthusiasm" that involves the whole person. She argues that, among intelligent women, the seat of love is not in the senses but in the head. Love "s'empare du cerveau d'abord, il frappe à la porte de l'imagination ... Il excite et subjugue toutes vos fibres vitales, j'en conviens, et les sens y jouent un grand rôle à leur tour. Mais la femme qui peut connaître le plaisir sans l'enthousiasme est une brute/overtakes the brain first, it strikes at the door of imagination...It excites and subjugates all our vital fibers, I admit it, and senses play a big part in their turn. But the woman who can know pleasure without enthusiasm is a brute." (722). What is surprising in Lucrezia's speech is both her acknowledgment of the role of physical pleasure in women's love and its limitations. Although nineteenth-century fiction recounts a number of love stories and affairs, there is hardly a discussion of the role of pleasure in women's relations. Sand's quiet acknowledgment (in fact much more scandalous than Lélia's admission of frigidity) recognizes women's access to the realm of physical pleasure while criticizing the separation of physical pleasure from other feelings. Although Sand's comments about pleasure without enthusiasm is limited to women, the reader cannot help feeling that women stand for men as well. The use of the word "brute" usually reserved for men suggests as much. While seeming to criticize women, Lucrezia (and Sand through her voice) is in fact criticizing men for their search for pleasure when it is unconnected to genuine emotional involvement. Indeed, Salvador will do exactly what Lucrezia says she rejects. He gets excited by the conversation, tries to kiss Lucrézia, and proposes a quick affair, which Lucrézia rejects immediately with the telling comment "I have no enthusiasm for you" and "Celui-là même qui a surpris les sens d'une femme n'a pas été son amant/The man who took a woman's senses by surprise has not been her lover" (728), reiterating the distinction she made between love (with sex) and sex without love. When Salvador expresses his regret at having offended her, Lucrézia's answer "Ma vie n'a pas été assez chaste pour que j'aie le droit de m'offenser d'un désir exprimé brutalement/My life hasn't been chaste enough for me to have the right to be offended by a desire expressed brutally" (728)), indicates that she understands the mechanics of male desire. Salvador, who is her friend and who presented her in the most positive of terms, unwittingly reveals that the difference of their views on love and pleasure has to do with power. Lucrézia rejects Salvador's view that what is spontaneous and irresistible (i.e., his sudden desire for her) is legitimate; on the contrary, she claims it is only the "right of the strongest" (728). Sand represents here two conceptions of desire that seem divided along gender lines: the ability to dissociate physical pleasure from emotional "enthusiasm' associated with the male characters, whereas the union of emotional involvement and sexual experience is associated with the woman character. However, as Lucrézia's comment also suggests, the difference in attitude has to do with power more than with inherent differences between men and women. She had also distinguished between "intelligent" women who don't experience pleasure without love and "brutes' (i.e., insensitive women who act like men).

However, Sand shows that her heroine's independence is diminished by her internalization of patriarchal symbolic representations. For all her savvy and her ability to distinguish between physical desire and love, Lucrezia has a conception of love that follow romantic images of love as an irrational passion that brings unhappiness (to women). Her conception of love as an initial enthusiasm that leads to disappointment is based on her failed affairs, one assumes. She states that love is a "sacrifice, torture and lassitude" (726). She tells Salvador that "quand tu te sentiras, toi, noble et honnête homme, violemment épris d'une misérable courtisane, sois certain que ce sera de l'amour et n'en rougis pas/when you feel, you a noble and honest man, violently taken by a miserable courtesan, be certain that it is love and don't be ashamed of it! " (725). Her conception of love is masochistic since it involves feelings for another person who is inferior and whose demands will destroy her peace. Her belief that love has nothing to do with the merit of the love object is tied to her invocation of Jesus for whom "love is greater in its cause than its object" (725). This selfless conception is strongly opposed by Salvador who objects that love is the most selfish of feelings (725). Here can be found the basic contrast between the sexes as represented by the characters. On the one hand, a conception of love as narcissistic desire where the loved one serves to reinforce the ego of the lover (which is the case for Salvador's affairs and for Prince Karol's expectations of Lucrezia); on the other, a conception of love as sacrifice of the person and unhappiness (a conception which is strangely close to that of the classical Lucrèce!).

However, Sand demonstrates how Lucrezia's pessimistic articulation of love relations is paradoxically linked to the degree of independence she displays in other areas of life. Throughout her professional and sentimental life, so the reader is told by the omniscient narrator, Lucrezia wants to remain independent and thus never had an affair with an aristocrat above her social station nor with a great artist (who would be her creative equal or superior). Thus she has chosen partners who are her inferior socially and intellectually [poor and obscure, as the narrator states (703)]. The problem seems that she also choses men who are inferior morally and who betray her in a variety of ways. Thus in her efforts to avoid occupying an inferior position in the love relation, Lucrezia reproduces an (inverted) inequality of positions.

Paradoxically, this inverted power structure is translated into her overemphasis on motherhood as a model structure for relations with men[19]. As we have seen, throughout the novel, she is presented as a "good" mother who cares deeply about her children, who fosters their creativity and who is willing to sacrifice her own desires in order to keep her children near her. Her maternal drive extends to her lovers, and her ill fated affair with Karol starts with her treating him like a child when she realizes that he is sick: "Je n'aime pas la sécheresse de cette main, dit-elle en interrogeant le poul de Karol, de cette petite main, car c'est la main d'une femme...*Che manina!*/I don't like the dryness of this hand, she said, as she felt Karol's pulse, of this little hand, for it is the hand of a woman, *Che manina!* " (734). Her comments reveal her ability to relate to men mostly from the powerful mother position. Although M-P. Rambeau has noted that in Sand the initial sensual impulse is triggered by the spectacle of fragility and suffering (291), Lucrezia's initial interest in Karol is definitely not sensual. When Karol falls ill, she nurses him as one of her children (735), the narrator tells us. Her nursing of Karol is the occasion for the narrator to describe and praise Lucrezia's understanding of matters of the body and illness. Seeing Karol, Lucrezia is reminded of Mrs Ranieri's illness: she"avait vu de ces phénomènes nerveux, et il lui suffisait de regarder les mains délicates du prince, sa peau blanche et transparente, ses cheveux fins et souples, un ensemble et des détails frappants, pour établir, entre lui et la maladie de Mme Ranieri des rapports qui ne trompent pas le coeur d'une femme/ had seen some of these nervous phenomena, and she only had to look at the delicate hands of the prince, this white transparent skin, this soft fine hair, an ensemble of striking details to establish between him and Mrs Ranieri's illness, relations that don't deceive the heart of a woman" (737). The description of Karol's body emphasizes his fragility, his child-like and feminized characteristics which contrast with Lucrezia's own strength and knowledge of the body and the mind, her power of observation and her nurturing savvy. Studies on the figure of the Romantic hero and his feminization have established that such feminization is presented as a negative move and that it does not entail a virilization of the female character[20], but Sand's play with gender construction reveals a different mode here: First, as we saw with *Jeanne*, Sand does not so much "virilize" her women characters as redefine and valorize traditional feminine associated traits. She thus take the "nurturing" or "maternal instinct" aspect and transforms it into a sign of strength and knowledge, and she distributes the trait among female and male characters (in this case, Salvador and Lucrezia) in a gesture that not only valorizes the traditional feminine but also destabilizes rigid gender lines. Likewise she takes traits like beauty or physical weakness or prudery and applies them to male characters (for instance, to Karol) in order to show that these traits are not inherent to a female subjectivity but are signs of specific gender positions. Thus, as we have seen, Sand takes great pain to redefine beauty when she applies it to Lucrezia in order to avoid placing her character in the position of object (of the male gaze or of desire).

However, Sand's representation of Lucrezia as a subject with agency also examines Lucrezia's reliance on the mother position, which reveals the power associated with being a mother, but also uncovers the weakness of this maternal model to accommodate the recognition of her identity and subjectivity. When Karol's passion for Lucrezia develops, the narrator uses a comparison that reveals the narcissistic position of the lover as child. Karol's love was "comme celui de l'enfant au berceau pour la femme qui l'allaite. Un attachement d'instinct, indissoluble et impérieux, s'empara de sa pauvre âme en détresse/like that of an infant for the woman who nurses him. An indissoluble and imperious instinctive attachment took over his poor soul" (739). This comparison suggests that Lucrezia's maternal approach to her relations with men has its dangers. Being like a mother does not mean so much being in the position of a protector who can control the relation as Lucrezia intimates, but being the target of an immature and demanding bond where the mother figure is effaced behind the love that consumes the masculine figure. Thus, when Karol suffers from fever during his illness, he takes Lucrezia for his mother (740) in a symbolic mistake: it is not that he has incestuous desires but that, as a mother figure, Lucrezia signifies the gratification of his needs without reciprocity. Karol's apparent weakness masks his unconscious desire to totally control her.

Here, Sand dramatically changes the terms of nineteenth-century discourse about women which invariably present them as unconscious or unknowing of their desires or feelings. Here it is the male character (metonymically the Romantic hero) who doesn't know what his love signifies.

As she does throughout the novel, Sand uses the narrator to tell the reader what will happen; Lucrezia will suffer and the affair will turn out badly. The narrator's comments suggest that what matters is not what happens (the Romantic passion scenario is too well-known) but how it will happen and by what mechanisms the heroine's suffering will occur. After commenting that Lucrezia had acted as the protector of the men she had loved, the narrator follows with a statement that self-imposed devotion inevitably leads to victimization (758). Contrary to the widespread nineteenth-century discourse on woman as having an instinct for self-sacrifice, the narrator's comment indicates that self-sacrifice is anything but natural (the "self" of "self-imposed" may suggest that the individual chose to devote herself but the "imposed" indicates that it is the opposite of a natural propensity). Sand uses the male discourse on woman and self-sacrifice but radically alters its meaning by linking it not to the "innate" morality of woman but to their being positioned as victims. As she did in *Gabriel*, Sand suggests that this victimization can be self-imposed and that women have agency even though this agency may be limited by the women's internalization of the norms of a patriarchal culture. Earlier in the novel, Lucrezia had told Salvador that she had left her last lover because of his insane jealousy and laughingly turned down Salvador's offer to protect her from him by reminding him that she was quite capable of protecting herself. (719). Lucrezia is shown to be able to protect her autonomy and to position herself in such a way that her desire to protect others does not necessarily mean that she can't be protected from them.

As she did in *Gabriel*, Sand thus presents a heroine whose negative narrative fate (her death) does not stem from her transgressions[21] but from her adherence to norms that configure woman as self-sacrificing and passive[22]. Lucrezia finally yields to her friend Salvador's attempt to throw Karol's into her arms with these words "Je l'aimerai...mais ce sera comme sa mère l'aimait/I'll love him...but as his mother did" (751). What she means is that she will be devoted to him and take care of him as she would her own children and that her feelings for him do not involve sexual desires. She explicitly rejects Karol as a possible lover. When Salvador pleads in his favor, she wonders why she is always the object of coarse desires ("désirs grossiers") using the same expression as when Salvador had suggested a quick affair. She further asks why she can't be treated like a "maternal friend" (744). For her maternal means outside the economy of male desire but, as the narrative comments indicate, men interpret the maternal not as meaning asexual but as narcissistic. It is this clash in the meaning of maternal and its consequences for her autonomy as a subject that Lucrezia fails to recognize and that leads to her demise. She comes to yield to the male definition of the maternal as a way to turn her strength and her propensity to protect into a selfless devotion to male needs. She will also accept to function as the one who fulfills the need of the lover-child, to give up her autonomy and to occupy the position of object of desire.

Although Lucrezia clearly articulates to Salvador her lack of interest in having love affairs (her previous experiences have brought her too many disappointments and unhappiness), she cannot sustain an asexual relation with Karol for long and she yields in part because Karol plays so well the role of the child as she conceives of it without realizing the danger (to her) of the relation. Karol is so dominated, so submissive (756) that Lucrezia thinks that she can control the direction of the relation, but as the narrator suggests, this apparent submission masks Karol's unconscious desire for power. He is described as a "doux et terrible enfant/sweet and terrible child" (755), and from child, he soon becomes a spoiled child, demanding her full attention at all times and alternating scenes of jealousy with meekness. Lucrezia does not treat his jealousy as an unacceptable pathology as she had with her previous lover (whom she had left) because their relation is based on a maternal model whereby the maternal figure attends to the suffering of the child figure (Karol) without being concerned for the results of such jealousy (that is her own unhappiness and suffering). Although the narrator describes Karol's jealousy as a pathology, rather than as the proof of the lover's depth of feeling as is customary in most nineteenth-century novels[23], Lucrezia's reaction is couched in terms of the maternal. In particular, when out of mental exhaustion she is on the verge of accepting Karol's offer of marriage (which he made in an attempt to control her completely), her situation is compared to that of a mother with a sick child who has been put on a severe diet by a doctor and who cries demanding food; the mother is tempted to yield to the child (808) and to trust nature's instinct (i.e., the child's desire) rather than the "rigor of science." The extended comparison is symbolic of the stakes at play: Karol's "natural instinct' is the desire to appropriate her and this desire is put in the context of an illness (jealousy). The comparison suggests that Lucrezia's survival as the mother is to refuse to give in this desire to assimilate her. But, of course, she will not.

The rest of the novel registers Karol's increasing jealousy and proprietary instinct and Lucrezia's slow death caused by his constant harassment. Karol's romantic passion devours Lucrezia whom he tortures paradoxically because she hides her suffering. Lucrezia does not understand that the mechanisms of jealousy involve the desire for power, precisely power over her; her refusal to resort to "feminine guile" (836) as the narrator calls the strategies of sulking and displaying anger, her very strength under duress spurs Karol on. The narrator mentions that Karol is jealous of her health and that if "si elle se fût montrée constamment à lui abattue et languissante, ou si elle eût pu affecter longtemps un air sombre et mécontent, elle l'eût guéri peut-être de sa personnalité maladive/she had showed herself to be downcast and despondent, or if she had been able to act somber and unhappy for a long while, she might have cured him of his pathological personality" (835). In other words, Lucrezia's suffering is caused by her inability to see Karol's behavior as symptomatic of an illness.

Here, Sand is not so much blaming the victim as showing that, for women, living freely and independently is not sufficient; if they have internalized at one level or another conceptions of love or desire that were constructed to benefit a male position, their independence on the economic or intellectual level will mean very little.

Like Gabriel, the character of Lucrezia serves to demonstrate that gender differences are constructed: by being and behaving both like a man and a woman, she belies the existence of natural differences. But by choosing to announce what will happen to her characters, and by focusing on the conditions that trigger the plot, Sand is able to uncover the way in which romantic desire is tied to a desire for power. By presenting Lucrezia as an eminently moral, yet sexual and conscious character, Sand offers a radical departure from the traditional contradictory representation of woman both as an asexual being or as a creature who cannot come to terms with her desires. In *Lucrezia*, it is the men who are not conscious of their desires. Karol, the feminized Romantic hero is sadly unaware of the fact that his passion for Lucrezia is the desire to appropriate the strength that he lacks. Salvador, Lucrezia's friend whose sexual advances she rejects, is not conscious of what he does when he uses his friendship with her to push his protégé Karol into her arms. Rather than considering her wishes to be left in peace, he works to satisfy the desires of his male friend and contributes to destroying her life. His alliance with Karol's narcissistic and destructive desires reveals his ultimate identification with the male position. Even though Salvador and Lucrezia share characteristics that expose the fragility of gender definitions (he displays positive "feminine" traits such as his nurturing capacity; Lucrezia is in many ways much more of a "man" than Karol in terms of strength, independence, activity), Salvador occupies a patriarchal position from which he can only conceive of woman as an object of desire and thus can only work to ensure that Lucrezia will become such an object. His opposition to Karol's sudden desire to marry Lucrezia reveals his awareness of the gulf that separates them:(he points out that Karol's age, rank, and personality cannot be compatible with "la fille d'un paysan, devenue comédienne, plus âgée que lui de six ans, mère de famille, démocrate dans ses instincts/the daughter of a peasant, turned actress, older by six years, a mother of four, democrat by instinct" (804); yet when Karol had everything to gain from his affair with Lucrezia, Salvador forgot these disparities. The issue of a possible marriage between the two, because it so obviously involves the two partners' class, property, descent, or "race' as Gabriel's grandfather would put it, reveals Salvador's class allegiance to the patriarchal order, which is linked to his unconscious alliance to the other male character. His participation in Lucrezia's victimization is thus inevitable as is Lucrezia's own self-victimization: the patriarchal ideology is so pervasive that no character can seem to escape it.

While Sand gives an ultimately pessimistic account of the power of the patriarchal order to exclude those who would question the foundation of the cultural category of gender, her extremely positive representation of the independent character Lucrezia and her suggestion that Lucrezia's demise is partly caused by her mistaken use of the maternal position as a model for heterosexual types of relation, indicate that women, once conscious of the arbitrariness of gender constructions, can come to occupy gender positions in which they will not be victimized, provided that they can extirpate from their inner beings the patriarchal values that they have internalized and that still cause their victimization. Sand's portrait of women who have crossed gender boundaries in *Gabriel* and *Lucrezia Floriani* already seems to suggest, in feminist Alice Jardine's words, that "To change the system, we have to change the speaking subject, but changing its gender or its cause is not sufficient. The subject must be thought in entirely new ways" (11).

NOTES

1. For a summary of Sand's efforts between 1851 and 1855 to have the play performed, see pp. 8-22 of Janice Glasgow's preface to *Gabriel*. Paris: Des Femmes, 1988.

2. Sand's foreword, which calls attention to her status as a mother, also protects her from prospective attacks stemming from the scandalous representation that is to follow: after all her heroine Gabriel has a long affair but never gets pregnant. Her sexual activity remains independent of the usual reproductive function of women. More significant perhaps is the fact that the only instances of fluid associated with Gabriel are the blood she sheds when she is stabbed at the end of the play. Sand never mentions or hints at menstrual blood, which would be a reassuring sign of Gabriel's position in the gender structure, in order to focus on that blood that is common to both men and women.

3. The use of the word "role" which refers both to the realm of nature and culture suggests that Sand intuits, contrary to the prevalent nineteenth-century view, that biology is never any more natural than culture, that as Thomas Laqueur has recently and brilliantly demonstrated in *Making Sex. Body and Gender From the Greeks to Freud,* the "so-called biological sex does not provide a solid foundation for the cultural category of gender, but constantly threatens to subvert it" (124). Cambridge: Harvard University Press, 1990.

4. As Joan Scott reminds us in *Only Paradoxes to Offer: French Feminists and the Rights of Man:* "by a kind of circular logic a presumed essence of men and women became the justification for laws and policies when, in fact, this 'essence' (historically and contextually variable) was only the effect of those laws and policies" (ix). Cambridge: Harvard University Press, 1996.

5. Bramante contrasts his affection for "the children of ma *race*" to the "childish worries of bourgeois fatherhood" (50).

6. In her account of transvestism in Renaissance England, Marjorie Garber shows that class and gender were revealed to be commutable, if not equivalent. To transgress against one set of boundaries was to call into question the inviolability of both. Obviously Bramante's violation of gender to preserve "race" or class will not be contained to that single category. Gabriel makes the connection between the two axes by referring to "la race male" (66). See Marjorie Garber, *Vested Interests. Cross-Dressing and Cultural Anxiety.* London: Routledge, 1992. Reprint New York: HarperCollins, 1993.

7. The recent review by Angeline Goreau of *Lieutenant Nun; Memoir of a Basque Transvestite in the New World* points out the same contradiction between Garber's interpretation of cross-dressing as a blurring of definitional distinctions and the fact that the cross-dresser in question conforms to the "most cliched version" of machismo. I would add also that Cataline de Erauso's story emphasizes her lack of sexual activity, as if the price for a woman's cross-dressing was the denial of sex. Rev. of *Lieutenant Nun,* by Cataline de Erauso, *New York Times* 17 Mar. 1996:28-29.

8. Judith Butler points out that "the category of sex belongs to a system of compulsory heterosexuality that clearly operates through a system of compulsory sexual reproduction." (*Gender Trouble* 111).

9. In her article on *Gabriel* Veronica Hubert-Matthews uses this dream as proof that Sand's presentation of femininity as constructed is also mixed in with hints of essentialism, but this interpretation does not take into consideration Gabriel's previous knowledge of her biological marking.

10. Of course, as Ann McCall has showed in "George Sand and the Genealogy of Terror," Astophe (a.k.a. Adolphe) is the prototypical Romantic hero deconstructed. *L'Esprit Créateur* 35.4 (1995): 38-48.

11. The situation in *Lucrezia Floriani* is similar. Lucrezia is the only woman in the novel. Her own mother died when she was an infant and Lucrezia Ranieri, her benefactress, died before Lucrezia became an adult. Moreover she seems to have no women friends. The only references to other women are to dead women (Karl's mother and his fiancee) who are responsible for constructing the male protagonist as a prototype egocentrist Romantic "hero." The absence of mothers in these two novels suggest that the gender ambiguities that the two heroines embody is possible because they haven't been socialized by mother figures whose traditional role in the patriarchy is to reproduce patriarchal structures.

12. As Ann McCall remarked during the May 1996 Sand Seminar held at Tuft University and organized by Isabelle Naginski, no mention is made of Gabriel menstruating, another sign that would definitely place her on the "female" side of the divide. By removing allusions to specific female functions (menstruation and reproduction), which usually serve as argument for the incommensurable difference existing between males and females, Sand seems to be questioning the biological basis for this difference.

13. For a thorough description of the role of Chopin in Sand's life and works (and in *Lucrezia Floriani* in particular), see M.P. Rambeau's *Chopin dans la vie et l'oeuvre de George Sand*. Paris: Les Belles Lettres, 1985.

14. Actually, Karol's friendship with Salvador is crucial, since Salvador is the only possible transition between the world of Karol and that of Lucrezia.

15. Sand had seen and commented approvingly on Ponsard's play *Lucrèce* (1843) in which his Lucrèce is the most moral of all the characters but also the most victimized. Sextus, the son of the tyrant Tarquin, wants to have her (in part because her husband has boasted of her beauty and virtue), and when she refuses, he rapes her. Lucrèce is so virtuous that she would prefer death, but Sextus tells her that if she doesn't submit, he will kill her and a slave that he will bring to her bed, then tell everyone that he found them together, thus ruining her reputation. Lucrèce thus submits, then tells what happened to her father and husband, making them promise to avenge her, and then commits suicide. As the plot summary indicates, Lucrèce is an incredibly strong character but all her strength is directed at preserving patriarchal values and leads to her death. See François Ponsard, *Lucrèce*. Paris: Calmann Lévy, 1894. The name of Lucrèce was so symbolic that it became a synonym for "virtuous woman," according to the Littré dictionary.

16. Her concern for her children was a source of irritation to A. de Pontmartin who reviewed *Lucrezia Floriani* in the *Revue des Deux Mondes* XVIII (1 April 1847). His plot summary emphasizes Karol's point of view and the impossibility of their love. The reviewer mentions in particular "her children are there, living memories, inexorable comments, and the diva displays a luxury of maternal feelings made to irritate a lover less resigned than Karol" (575). In other words, the realms of motherhood and romantic love should be kept separate.

17. Sand gave the same explanation for her move from Paris to Nohant. She wanted to protect Maurice and Solange from gossip about her life.

18. Here, we can understand why Sand denied having used Chopin as a model for Karol as the whole critique of the male character centers on his inactivity and his lack of creativity, characteristics without which Chopin was no longer Chopin. Sand is showing how lack of involvement in the world of work or of mature emotions is detrimental both to women (who are traditionally excluded from this world) and to men.

19.Sand is known for having engaged in relationships with men younger and weaker than she was, Chopin, for instance. However, as her long affair with Chopin shows, there was certainly an equality socially and intellectually or creatively and the relation did not turn masochistic. When Chopin's jealousy became overbearing, Sand broke off with him, which is precisely what Lucrezia Floriani fails to do with her abusive lover.

20. That is, for instance, what Margaret Waller has shown in *The Male Malady: Fictions of Impotence in the French Romantic Novel* in particular about Chateaubriand's *René*. New Brunswick: Rutgers University Press, 1993.

21. Among other things, her having eloped with the son of her benefactress, her having been a successful actress and dramatist, her having had several affairs, and her having had four children out of wedlock and from different fathers.

22. For an interesting discussion of the ways woman was configured in nineteenth-century discourse as naturally moral and self-sacrificing, see Mary Poovey, "Speaking of the Body: Mid-Victorian Construction of Female Desire." Pp. 29-46 in Mary Jacobus, Evelyn Fox Keller, Sally Shuttleworth, eds. *Body/Politics. Women and the Discourse of Science.* London: Routledge, 1990.

23. For a discussion of the representation of jealousy as an homage to the woman protagonist in a number of male writers' fiction, see M-P Rambeau's discussion in *Chopin dans la vie et l'oeuvre de George Sand* 321-322.

CHAPTER V
NANON AND UTOPIAS OF GENDER

Sand's exploration of the construction of gender identities ended with the publication of *Nanon* (1872), the last novel she was to write in its entirely before her death[1] (1876). Sand's life long reflection ends with an optimistic note: unlike her other heroines Jeanne, Gabriel or Lucrezia Floriani, her protagonist Nanon lives a long happy autonomous life that bears witness to her energy and cultural power. In *Nanon* Sand offers her most thorough problematization of gender differences and of the patriarchal erotics of female frailty. *Nanon* intensifies the themes and strategies present in the earlier novels but its utopian description of equality and partnership of the couple Nanon and Emilien de-emphasizes sexuality as an issue in the reconfiguration of male/female relations. Sand's lack of interest in depicting sexual drives may be linked to biographical factors (she was sixty eight when she wrote *Nanon* and sexual matters may have seemed less pressing) or may be an expression of the "reterritorialization of female sexuality unto maternity" as Reid has argued about nineteenth-century family narratives, but I will suggest that her lack of interest in depicting feminine sexual desires is an ultimate attempt to draw attention to the fact that the realm of the sexual is ultimately cultural, and that separating sexual desire from other kinds of desires helps reproduce a traditional patriarchal hegemony.

Nanon is now a fairly well-known novel. It recounts the life of a young orphaned peasant girl Nanon during the Revolution as she befriends and is befriended by a young monk, Emilien de Franqueville, the youngest son of an aristocratic family who has all but abandoned him. The novel registers Nanon's gradual access to power as she becomes literate, manages and buys property that once belonged to the Church, saves her friend Emilien from the Terror, then accumulates land while waiting for him to return from the revolutionary wars. After his return (he is maimed but alive), they marry and live happily ever after.

Nanon's depiction of a life spanning most of the century and especially the troubled times of the French Revolution has begun to be mentioned in a number of studies.[2] Doris Kadish has showed that *Nanon*'s representation of marriage as the locus for power relations was a way to represent collective issues (thereby to conflate the public and the private sphere, an important move since the dominant nineteenth-century bourgeois ideology is based on the absolute separation of the spheres[3]), while Naomi Schor has noted that *Nanon* represents the constitution of a new national identity "based on a contractual rather than a blood relation between individuals" (Schor 153). In her introduction to her edition of *Nanon*, Nicole Mozet has also pointed out that although it is not a realist novel, it has much to say about the historical and social historical reality of the nineteenth-century. [4]

Sand's representation of the political revolution of 1789 is crucial for our understanding of the forces at work at the beginning of the nineteenth-century, but her description of the revolution also masks another revolution that involves gender and in which binary opposites between the feminine and the masculine are blurred. Gender is presented as a performance linked to specific cultural contexts. The powerful pre-revolutionary sado-masochistic model represented in the famous novel *Manon (Lescault)* is discarded, not in favor of the revolutionary image of the Republican mother or the hegemonic bourgeois model of woman as frail creature governed by laws of "nature,"[5] but by a utopian model of partnership and mutual nurturing.[6]

As Sand did in her previous novels, she uses a narrator that cannot be trusted. Although the narrator is Nanon, the empowered heroine of the novel, and although the novel uses a first person narration[7], Sand makes sure from the beginning that the readers will not be threatened by the presence of an all-powerful female who both controls the story and is its main protagonist. The narrative of Nanon's life begins with an apology explaining that her goal is not to focus on her story but to preserve the memory of her husband for her children and grandchildren (31). Of course, the whole narrative is constituted by her version of history and does recount her story. The strategy of modesty which will be repeated at other moments in the novel masks the strangeness of having history both personal and national (private and public) presented, interpreted, and acted by a woman from the peasantry in stark contrast with the dominant image of French national culture as male, Parisian, and Bourgeois.

To further mask the power and knowledge behind Nanon's narrative act, Sand has her add "Je ne sais pas si je pourrai raconter par écrit, moi qui, à douze ans, ne savais pas encore lire/ I do not know if I'll be able to write my story; at twelve I could not yet read" (31). This remark, innocuous as it seems, is disingenuous since the narrative that follows is precisely the narrative of her access to symbolic language and to the written word in particular. Not only can she write, she can also evaluate the writing of others (she comments on the poor spelling of the aristocratic Louise, Emilien's sister), she can read maps, and she masters the codes legislating writing (she forges signatures and documents during the reign of Terror to save her friend Emilien). Thus, Nanon's modest stance is a strategy to call the reader's attention away from the cultural scandal constituted by her act of writing and of looking. By making Nanon the narrator and the focalizer, Sand changes the dynamics of the gaze that is common to most nineteenth-century narratives, be they Romantic or realist narratives. Instead of having women characters who express the fantasies of the male author or of a male narrator, Sand shifts the point of view to a woman who is not an embodiment of the patriarchy. Through that shift, Sand blurs gender differences, and offers a critique of male desire by focusing on the reactions of the woman subject as she discovers her objectification.

Nanon's narrative disclaimer makes her story culturally acceptable and makes her invisible as a woman. When speaking of herself, she avoids using the word "femme" to avoid being categorized and dismissed by nineteenth-century patriarchal discourses about women and femininity. Nanon's initial reluctance to name herself as woman is part of Sand's attempt to show that femininity is a cultural performance that can vary according to a number of factors (class, ethnicity, etc). Nanon speaks of herself as a "personne" and when she recounts her early confused memories, she uses the word "enfant/child" rather than girl. Furthermore, the narrative focuses on the similarities between her and the boy Emilien. Sand is not denying that there are biological women and men, but she wants to avoid having her heroine's experience dismissed because she is a girl. By focusing on Nanon as a human being before defining her as a woman, she will be able to describe the cultural mechanisms of "engendering" and question the hierarchy of sexual difference.

Sand uses physical description to question the hierarchy of sexual difference. Nanon does not describe herself in any detail (all we know is that she had smallpox and was homely (90) until she is eighteen when her physical attractiveness becomes a textual issue in the context of unwelcome reactions to it). The physical description of Emilien given by Nanon emphasizes common traits rather than gender differences, and at the same time, embodies an egalitarian politics of the gaze. The first description is revealing "Je vis...une jeune et douce figure de novice qui me regardait en riant/I saw...the young and sweet face of a novice who was looking at me and laughing"(37). This short description expresses the ideal of equality and partnership that structures the plot of the novel. Both the narrator and the character are observers as well as objects of the observation; both direct their gaze in a non-aggressive way. The terms used by Nanon "young and sweet face"could apply to a male as well as to a female. These details, like the reciprocal focus of the subjects suggest similarities rather than difference. The rest of the details provided by Nanon also emphasize similarities. Emilien has a "soft voice"(39), which does not mark him as specifically masculine; and he is physically active "car il était fort, quoique d'apparence chétive/for he was strong although he seemed rather puny"(45).

The contrast between apparent weakness and actual strength is also a characteristic of Nanon, and is meant to convey that physical size is not correlated to any sexual superiority. Nanon describes herself in almost similar terms "quoique maigre et chétive d'apparence, je devins vite très forte et presque infatigable/although I was skinny and looked puny, I quickly became quite strong and almost indefatigable"(35). As with Emilien's case, these comments indicate that her strength is a consequence of her physical activity and thus undermine beliefs in biological fate. Of course, Sand acknowledges the existence of specific physical differences between male and female characters but she rejects the negative meaning assigned to characteristics of the female body. For instance, instead of being a sign of weakness, smallness of size is interpreted as an advantage when it allows Nanon to enter the cell where Father Fructueux is imprisoned (76). Similarly, when her cousin mocks her for having very small hands and feet, her mentor Mariotte points out that size is irrelevant; what counts is endurance. And sure enough, when Nanon has to walk for two days to find out where Emilien is kept prisoner, her feet hold up (120). In other words, physical differences between the sexes need not be translated into inferiority.

The last details Nanon gives about Emilien also blur distinctions between the masculine and the feminine, and between the physical and the moral. She hears him call her name and sees him: "Il me parut le plus joli du monde. Et pourtant il n'était pas beau, mon pauvre cher Franqueville, mais son air était si bon, il avait des yeux si clairs et un visage si doux.../He seemed to be the most beautiful of all; and yet my poor dear Franqueville was not handsome, but he looked so kind, his eyes were so clear and his face so sweet that..."(44). The description dismisses inherent physical beauty as a relevant measure of human beings's worth and thus questions the cultural emphasis on beauty as a way to assess women's worth. The downplay of physical beauty may not seem surprising because the character described is male (and beauty is not a cultural requirement for masculinity), but the terms of the description (joli, doux) evoke traditional feminine characteristics and, by extension , the description indirectly questions the importance of physical beauty for women, a question which Sand will take up later when she represents male reactions to Nanon's attractiveness. Sand does not feminize the male character; she questions the adequacy of patriarchal sexual prejudices to account for differences in people. The physical descriptions of the two protagonists indicate that they exist in a space beyond strict gender boundaries, a space made possible in part by their isolation, which emphasizes once again that for Sand sex and gender are culturally constructed.

In *Nanon*, as in a number of Sand's novels (*Indiana, Jacques, Gabriel, La petite Fadette, Consuelo*, among others), children are orphaned literally or symbolically and traditional family structures are no longer in place[8]. The lack of parents, which may appear as a loss, also provides a space for the children to develop without having to conform to rigid social and sexual models. For instance, Nanon is free to roam the countryside, to develop a friendship with someone of a different class, and doesn't have to follow established models of feminine behavior. She is brought up mostly among men by a grand uncle who is widowed and lives with her male cousins. The only female influence is that of a neighbor woman "une très bonne et honnête femme/a very good and honest woman" who gives her advice. This woman is widowed, which means that she is self-reliant and outside a direct patriarchal system of control as well. She lives alone, survives although she is very poor and teaches Nanon how to be resourceful. The qualities that she encourages in Nanon—honesty, hard work, clear thinking—are not linked to traditional conceptions of femininity or masculinity.

The figure of the grand uncle appears patriarchal but doesn't share a number of the prejudices usually associated with patriarchy: he is the authority figure in the household; but, interestingly, his authority seems to reside in his age and wisdom rather than in his being a male. Moreover, the fact that he is two generations apart from Nanon and not a direct ascendant suggests a distance from the symbolic weight of a traditional father figure. The details given about his attitude toward Nanon emphasize his nurturing (Nanon recalls his affectionate gestures "il me caressait parfois le dimanche/sometimes on Sundays he would treat me with gestures of affection" (31). He encourages Nanon to become independent and links her development as a woman to specific actions. In an effort to participate in the chores, Nanon attempts to make soup for the whole household amidst the taunts of her older male cousins, but her uncle sees that as a responsible gesture and comments on her maturity "Puisque te voilà une femme/now that you are a woman" (33). For him, to be a woman or to have become a woman is to behave responsibly; it is the opposite of being like a child. To reward her, the uncle gives her a ewe to take care of. Through this simple incident, Sand provides a correction to the dominant bourgeois view of women as childlike creatures who need protection. On the contrary, she shows that women, at least in the peasantry she describes, are "women" (as opposed to children) because they can contribute to the support of the family and be full partners.[9]

The importance of an occupation to moral development is stressed by Nanon herself. As soon as she is responsible for the ewe, Nanon feels that she is a whole person "Je sentis que j'étais quelqu' un... J'avais une occupation, un devoir, une responsabilité, une propriété, dirai-je une maternité, à propos d' un mouton/ I felt that I was someone... I had an occupation, a duty, a responsibility, a property, a maternity so to speak, about a sheep" (34). Revealingly, Nanon conceives of herself as a "person" an inclusive term, rather than a woman, a term that is exclusive and that defines human beings in ways that emphasize the determinism of their biological sex rather than the shared characteristics of people. Through Nanon's reflection on responsibility, Sand thus suggests that we need to think of women as human beings who as such need for their development the same opportunity to be responsible as do men. The list of nouns given by Nanon to describe what was necessary for her to feel human—occupation, duty, responsibility, property, maternity—by the fact of their contiguity suggests synonymity and continuity.

Thus, maternity becomes parallel to responsibility and occupation. To have an occupation is to feel a "maternity." By putting on the same plane terms which were considered incommensurate, Sand is undoing the familiar binary opposition which separate the male and the female realm, the cultural and the biological. By conflating the moral and the social (duty and property), the mental and the physical (responsibility and maternity), she is suggesting that we need to think of biological and cultural differences as differences on a scale rather than as set of absolute oppositions. She is not denying difference; she is questioning the significance given to specific differences. At the same time, by putting maternity on the same plane as responsibility and occupation, she is suggesting that in order to be fully human, women need to have access to occupations as well as to maternity. Nanon's seemingly naive attempt to describe her sense of becoming a person undermines the nineteenth-century dominant discourse which defined maternity as the only realm where a woman's sense of responsibility could be experienced.

Nanon's articulation of the importance for women of being responsible and active to be human will be further developed when Sand describes the fate of Louise, a woman who is dehumanized because she does not have any responsibility or occupation. Sand will show how self-destructive it is for prejudiced men (as represented by the revolutionary Costejoux) to remain attached to images of femininity that deny women their humanity.

Sand's representation of Nanon's childhood is the occasion to describe a process by which specific roles are learned and to use the lack of a traditional family structure founded on the opposition of the feminine and the masculine to allow the characters to move into a variety of positions (because there is no feminine figure, the grand-uncle can be nurturing; because she is a poor widow, the neighbor is self-sufficient like a "man"). In her previous novels, Sand had showed how an older generation enforced strict gender and class divisions but in *Nanon* she shows what can happen when such a force is absent. The utopian aspect of Nanon's access to responsibility and power is further facilitated by her uncle's death during the revolution, which removes the last authority figure that could control her.[10]

Sand's presentation of the influence of cultural models for the construction of gender follows the same pattern with the male character Emilien. Although he is not an orphan at the beginning of the novel, he has been abandoned by his family in a convent so that his elder brother can inherit the whole family fortune. Besides presenting a criticism of the French aristocracy's custom of primogeniture, Emilien's situation provides an explanation for specific lacks in children of the upper classes and is a way to free Emilien from aristocratic models and prejudices. When Nanon questions Emilien about his parents and his feelings for them, he answers that he hardly knows them (40) and implies that he cannot love what he doesn't know. The result of Emilien's abandonment and lack of bonding with family members is that he expects nothing from life and has become emotionally and intellectually numb until Nanon teaches him to care about others. Sand's description of Emilien's situation, like that of Nanon, emphasizes the role of a nurturing environment for the development of individuals. She rejects the emphasis on "nature" whether applied to gender or to class.

The only exception to Emilien's indifference to others is the love he claims for his younger sister Louise, the only family member with whom he had contacts. His concern for his sister will be displayed later during the reign of the Terror when he rescues her from the clutches of dishonest servants, but strangely enough, the novel fails to portray convincingly any scene of brotherly interaction as if Emilien's sister was brought in merely for plot reasons and to further exemplify the result of specific cultural practices. The failure to represent a brotherly relation parallels the historical failure of the fraternal model. Although Lynn Hunt has argued that the pre-revolutionary model of a family hierarchy headed by the father was replaced by a fraternal structure, there is little evidence in nineteenth-century history of this new model as Maurice David's studies of fraternity suggest[11]. As Allan Pasco argues[12], "no such chronology leading from loveless tyrannical paternity to feckless fatherhood, to brotherhood can be sustained;" and Sand's novel registers the elusiveness of this structure by representing fraternal relations (be they religious or family fraternal relations) that are named but absent.

However, the presence of Louise has other purposes besides representing the myth of fraternal relations; it allows Sand to question the nineteenth-century revolutionary and bourgeois construct of the aristocratic woman as agent of decay in French culture. She presents Louise as a selfish, prejudiced, and ignorant girl, but suggests that these defects are the result, not of innate qualities, but of specific cultural practices that make indifference a condition for survival. Sand explains the causes and consequences of the lack of parental affection: "Sa mère ne l'avait jamais caressée, et, sachant qu'il faudrait se séparer d'elle le plus tôt possible et pour toujours, elle s'était défendu de l'aimer...son [Louise] coeur n'avait pas de tendresse/her mother had never treated her with gestures of affection, and, knowing that she would have to leave her at the earliest possible and forever, she had refrained from loving her...her[Louise] heart had no tenderness" (91). Sand carefully uses the same word "caresser" that she had used previously to describe Nanon's relation with her grandfather (31) to suggest a comparison between the two situations. Nanon is an orphan but she has an extended family who nurtures her. In contrast, Louise has a mother who ignored her not because she is a cold woman or because she is busy with court appearances but because the cultural fate of aristocratic daughters is to be separated from their mothers and to be bartered into another family. Indifference is necessary to survive inevitable separation. Sand thus presents both aristocratic mother and daughter as victims of specific class practices.[13]   Sand uses these characters to demonstrate how the patriarchal family (which embodies specific class and gender values) structures the most basic relations of individuals to each other. In the case of Louise, it means learning selfishness from a mother who is of necessity a non-nurturing and an absent mother in conformity with the requirements of her class.

The fraternal bond in its literal sense is emptied of its meaning because in part Louise is showed to be incapable of bonding with anyone. Then Nanon's use of the fraternal model as a metaphor for friendship is similarly empty: it is not based on existing biological relations as we have seen with Emilien and Louise, nor on institutional relations (the "Brothers" of the convent share little but their exclusion from society, and turn against each other[14]). When Nanon invokes the fraternal bond to describe her relation with Emilien "nous nous aimions comme si la même mère nous eût mis au monde/ we loved each other as if we had the same mother" (91), she is referring to a mythical family since she only knows instances of families where the mother is dead or absent and where siblings show little love (even in the case of her own two cousins who don't seem to care much for her and who are prejudiced). The fraternal metaphor, however, does allow her to allude to a new kind of heterosexual relation that she renders acceptable by removing from it a double taboo: the general taboo of incest—if her relation with Emilien is a brotherly relation, then the sexual is removed from the affective bond; and the taboo of class mingling—if her relation is brotherly, they will not get married and disturb the strict hierarchical structure of nineteenth-century French society. Presenting this relation based on equality (which crosses class as well as gender lines) as a fraternal relation is a way to coopt the Revolutionary rhetoric of fraternity, an idea, which although part of the post-revolutionary French mentalité, never became actualized, and to carve a space for a new type of relation not modeled on what men desire.

Nanon's early exclusion of sexual desire from "love" stems also from a rejection of a male erotics model that is based on unequal power and that victimizes women. In this regard, Sand's presentation follows the pattern that she developed in *Indiana*, *Jeanne*, or even *Gabriel*. The difference is that in *Nanon*, the heroine can escape victimization and write the script of a new kind of relation. In *Nanon*, most heterosexual relations follow a sadomasochistic model in with both partners are victimized or the woman is threatened. This model is developed in the representation of the relation between the revolutionary lawyer Costejoux and Louise, Emilien's aristocratic sister. Their relation begins when Louise is still a spoiled child in an episode in which Nanon describes and explains her arrogance and its effects on Costejoux. Louise's appeal to Costejoux is based on the fact that he is all powerful but she challenges him (and, of course, she is noble and pretty). Nanon's narrative reveals the extreme disparity of power between the two and the underlying violence of the relation: "il s'amusa toujours de ces façons de souveraine. Plus il était ennemi de la noblesse, plus il trouvait divertissant de voir ce petit rejeton incorrigible qu' il eut pu écraser entre ses doigts lui sauter à la figure et lui donner des ordres/he always enjoyed her queenly manners. The more he opposed the aristocracy, the more he found amusing to see the little incorrigible offspring, whom he could have squashed between his fingers, fly to his throat and give him orders" (93). The references to violent acts (écraser/squash, sauter à la figure/fly to his throat) and to class relations based on power (souveraine, noblesse, rejeton) show that for the male revolutionary Costejoux equality is strictly limited to the political. In fact, he reinscribes in the realm of the personal the worst aspects of pre-revolutionary inequalities. His own account of his relation with Louise suggests that the revolution may have changed the class that has power but that it has kept intact the power structure and the violence associated with it. As Costejoux explains to Nanon: "il y a comme un irrésistible besoin d'abdiquer dans l'intimité de la famille et d'oublier que l'on est terroriste, pour se laisser terroriser à son tour, ne fût-ce que par les coups de bec d'un petit oiseau/there is like an irrésistible need to surrender within the intimacy of the family circle and to forget that one is a terrorist, to allow oneself to be terrorized in one's turn, if only by the pecks of a little bird" (188). His comparing Louise to a frail bird after stating that she is "une femme, une vraie femme, avec toutes les séductions et toutes des fantaisies de la faiblesse/she is a woman, a true woman, with all the seductions and the whimsy of weakness" (188) and in the same sentence the terms "surrender," "terrorist" reveal the limit of Costejoux's ability to change, and the reasons for Nanon's refusal to accept to submit to sexual laws as they are still defined.   The revolutionaries's successful attempt to silence women politically is now well-known, but here Sand describes the private mechanisms that supported post-revolutionary public policies and allowed gender roles to reflect the very inequalities and exclusions that the French revolution had sought to modify in the realm of social classes.

Sand comments further on the revolutionaries' failure to redefine gender roles according to principles of equality. When Costejoux is disappointed in the direction taken by the revolution, he blames women from the nobility—a now familiar move—arguing that the *Tiers Etat* is becoming corrupt because it "singe la noblesse et la fréquente, les femmes de cette race nous subjuguent/ mimic nobility associate with its member; the women of this race subjugate us" (233). Instead of blaming the men who wield power for failing to conceive of relations other than power relations based on the constructed weakness of one of the parties, he reverts to the irrational: the revolutionaries are "subjugated."

Costejoux's account of his dedication to the Revolution uses the same sadomasochistic terms he had used earlier to describe his relation to

Louise: "J'aimais la Révolution comme on aime une amante. Pour elle, j'aurais de mes mains arraché mes entrailles/I loved the Revolution like a lover. For it, I would have torn away my entrails" (232). The violent love/sex metaphor (the idea that the ultimate devotion is self-mutilation, the projection of the responsibility of the male desire unto the women expressed by words like "subjuguer," which explicitly link seduction and power) all reveal a conception of affective/sexual relations and politics that are linked to pre-revolutionary Sadian fantasies.

Another instance of Sand's representation of the revolutionary adoption of sado-masochistic models is her description of the revolutionary festival during which a woman dressed as a Goddess frightens a bourgeois suspected of royalist loyalties into kneeling in the street and being used as her stepping stool. Although Naomi Schor has read this episode as Sand's negative presentation of women who play a public role, the previous analysis about Costejoux's patriarchal revolutionary ideology suggests that what Sand criticizes is not so much women in a public role but the adoption by the Revolution of a sexual model that relies on inequalities and on the objectification and debasement of one of the partners.

Sand further questions the logic of the revolutionaries's patriarchal stance on the issue of the responsibility of women from the aristocracy or who served the aristocracy when Nanon laments the beheading of the queen in seemingly naive terms: "Pourquoi faire mourir une femme? disais-je, quel mal peut-elle avoir fait? N'était-ce pas à elle d'obéir à son mari et de penser comme lui?/Why condemn a woman? I would say, what harm could she have done? Wasn't it her role to obey her husband and to think like him? (154)" Nanon's argument is the logical conclusion of the patriarchal view that women are inferior and must obey men. If this is the case, of course, they bear no responsibility of any kind, and the revolutionary and post revolutionary hatred of women of the nobility is without foundation. By having Nanon articulate the patriarchal view in a way that reveals its self-contradictions Sand forces her readers to distance themselves from such a view and then, through Emilien's mouth (as a man from the nobility who rejects the prejudices of his class, he does not threaten the readers and has authority) she counters that the queen was responsible for her actions and deserves the guillotine more than an ignorant servant put to death for things she did not understand. Emilien suggests that class differences (linked to power and knowledge) matter more than gender differences. He further expresses the view that husbands often obey their wives and that it is right when the wives think more clearly (154). In other words, he rejects the claim that women think less rationally than men, a view which has already been expressed indirectly by Nanon's question. The price that Sand pays for the strategy of using her powerful woman narrator to voice the most extreme patriarchal view only to have it immediately undermined by another unthreatening character is a certain lack of consistency. Like Nanon's initial narrative stance, these occasional patriarchal comments contrast with Nanon's actions and with the ideological underpinnings of the novel, but they allow Sand to present a critique of patriarchal prejudices that will not be easily rejected.

The revolutionaries's inability to relinquish the master/slave model that structures gender relations explains Nanon's reluctance to conceive of her relations with Emilien as "love" relations since the concept of love is embedded in a web of social practices that deny most women agency and equality.

Sand emphasizes that, generally, expressions of male desires are oppressive to women by presenting all the encounters that Nanon has with men and their desires as an aggression and a threat. In her attempt to save Emilien from jail, she goes to Costejoux's headquarters and her encounter with his acolytes, who are rough characters, frightens her. She recoils when one of them who finds her pretty "me posa sur la joue une grosse main velue qui me fit peur. Mais j'avais à jouer un rôle et je cachai mon dégoût/lay on my cheek a big hairy hand which frightened me. But I had to play my part and I hid my disgust" (115). The unwelcome touching is a revealing example of the way men's desires are experienced by women, especially when they have little social power, a theme that we have seen in

Sand's earlier novels. The men's reactions to Nanon are triggered by her attractiveness and Nanon suddenly realizes that her beauty (i.e., the traditional symbol of femininity) is a liability. Costejoux himself comments that Nanon used to be homely but that she has become pretty. When Nanon rejects his comment by asking why would that matter (119), Costejoux just calls her "petite amoureuse/little lover" which offends her. The implication is that her actions stem from an infatuation with Emilien rather than from loyalty, courage, and friendship, qualities that are much less gendered than love. The terms of her denial reveal the reasons for her reluctance to think of love. She replies "je n'ai pas l'âge de l'amour et je suis un coeur honnête/I am not old enough for love and I am an honest heart" (118). Her reference to age has more to do with her lack of readiness than with biological age since she is eighteen at the time. As a country girl she is obviously familiar with the facts of life, so it is not ignorance or innocence on her part but lack of interest.

Secondly, the reference to honesty implies that she is aware of the social gap between her and Emilien and that the only option for her if she was to act on her "being in love" with him would be to become his mistress. Thus Nanon's refusal to conceive of her relation with Emilien as a love relation (and thus as a sexualized relation) is a strategy to preserve the equality that structures their relation and to claim her right to remain a child, that is a person whose identity is not dependent on her relations to the opposite sex.

Her refusal to be defined as an object of men's desire and her sense of the danger inherent to being such an object is expressed in several ways. First, she realizes that men notice her; therefore her movements will be constrained and she won't be able to act discreetly to save Emilien. When she gets a ride on the carriage leading the prisoners to another town (Emilien is among them and she hopes to be able to help him escape), the driver comments on her looks (125) and she perceives his reactions as a hindrance to her freedom "Je voyais enfin dans mon sexe un obstacle et des périls auxquels je n'avais jamais songé! La pudeur se révèlait sous forme d'effroi...La beauté attire toujours les regards et j'aurais voulu être invisible/Last, I saw in my sex an obstacle and dangers about which I had never thought! I discovered modesty as dread...Beauty always attracts looks and I wished I could have been invisible ." (125).

Beyond the real danger of being sexually attacked by one of the unscrupulous terrorists leading the prisoners, she realizes that being identified as a woman alone is dangerous. To avoid this danger, she wears boy's clothing, which allows her to become "invisible." The verbal invisibility that she sought in her narrative stance and which, removed from its context, can be interpreted as a form of subservience[15], is paralleled by her move to physical invisibility. Here the desire for invisibility stems from the realization that being perceived as a woman (which in turn hinges on being pretty) leads to being treated as an object of desire that men will want to "have" rather than "being" a free agent. Nanon is learning that, in the world of men, being a woman is not the positive experience that it was in her peasant family (where womanhood signified responsibility, partnership and autonomy). In this context being a woman means becoming an object defined in terms of the effect it has on men.

Sand's representation of patriarchal men's desire as a narcissistic reaction to women's physical attributes is further developed in an incident during which Costejoux, who realizes that Nanon would make a better mate than Louise, tells Nanon "je vois en toi un esprit supérieur, un caractère admirable. Tu es assez belle pour que l'on te désire et, si tu m'encourageais, j'oublierais facilement tout ce qui n'est pas toi/ I see in you a superior mind, an admirable personality. You are pretty enough to be desired and, if you were to encourage me, I would easily forget everything that is not you"(193). Of course, Nanon rejects his offer, which reveals once again that her superior moral and intellectual qualities are attractive to Costejoux only because she is also pretty. That desire is born in the desiring man rather than in inherent characteristics of the object of desire is revealed in the terms used by Costejoux: rather than focusing on Nanon, he stresses his own perceptions of her. She is not just superior; *he* sees her as superior. She is not simply pretty; *on* (i.e., men) desire her. In the context of Costejoux's later diatribe against aristocratic women whom he blames for subjugating men, his comments to Nanon show how difficult it is to move beyond patriarchal modes of desire. He realizes that his prejudiced views of the female sex are inadequate when confronted by someone like Nanon (He tells her "Vous êtes une exception, vous, une très remarquable exception. Vous n'êtes ni une femme ni un homme, vous êtes l'un et l'autre avec les meilleures qualités des deux sexes[16]/ You are an exception, a quite remarkable exception. You are neither a woman nor a man; you are both with the best qualities of both sexes"(188), but the cultural forces that shape his views of sexual differences are such that he cannot let go of his prejudices.[17]

With her portrait of Costejoux, Sand shows the disconnection between political radicalism and enlightened views about sex and gender, and expresses her doubts about the possibility of changes brought about by an intervention in the public space when it is not accompanied by changes within the individual.[18] However, with the figure of Emilien, she provides a character who expresses his radicalism in the public sphere (he abandons the privileges of his class by enrolling in the French revolutionary army) as well as in the private sphere by rejecting rigid gender boundaries and oppressive modes of desiring.

Nanon's instinctive refusal to become objectified explains why she cannot realize that Emilien loves her and why he does not speak his love. After she successfully saves him from jail, they go hide in a deserted place with Emilien's former servant Dumont and live peacefully, if frugally. When at one point Emilien kisses her hands with joy (and thus expresses his love), she interprets his gesture according to a mythic family narrative which allows her to dismiss the implications of his gesture. She does not resort to the fraternal model, but she uses the other available model; that is the mother, which is as inadequate as the sister figure to articulate the new type of relation she seeks. Emilien's kiss was a response to Nanon's surprise that he did not list her when he thanked the friends who helped him escape and survive. He tells her that their bond is of a different kind. Her lack of understanding at what he means makes him laugh and, rather than confronting her with his feelings, he kisses her hand, which she interprets as follows : "il se mit à rire en couvrant mes mains de baisers comme si j'eusse été sa mère/he started laughing, kissing my hand all over as if I had been his mother"(149). Emilien's reaction shows he respects Nanon's refusal to face his love: "sois ma mère, je veux bien, car je me figure que, si j'en avais eu une véritable, je n'aurais aimé qu'elle au monde. Prends donc pour toi tout le respect, toute la tendresse, toute l'adoration que j'aurais eu pour elle/all right, be my mother, because I figure that if I had had a real mother, she would have been my only love. Take for yourself all the respect, the affection, the adoration that I would have felt for her"(149). Although Schor has stated that Nanon becomes Emilien's symbolic mother (134), this exchange shows that Nanon uses the mother figure as a way to avoid being an object of Romantic love, and thus to become the inferior partner, while Emilien deconstructs the reference to the mother and accepts to use it out of respect for Nanon. Nanon later recalls this exchange but she revealingly misattributes the reference to the mother: "Une fois il m'avait appelé sa mère, et il est bien vrai que je le considerais comme mon enfant, en même temps que comme le maître de ma vie et la lumière de mon âme/Once he had called me his mother, and it is quite true that I felt he was my child, and at the same time the master of my life and the light of my soul"(172). Unlike other nurturing characters in Sand's earlier fiction (for instance Lucrezia Floriani), Nanon is not victimized by male character's demands that she indulge their narcissistic needs. The "mothering" she claims is a mutual nurturing that benefits her as much as Emilien, who is precisely the one who did not ask her to be his mother.

That Emilien is capable of holding his desire in check and of keeping his romantic love silent or at least to couch it in non threatening ways suggests that he is aware of the politics of desire and that he strives for an egalitarian mode where the desires of men correspond to the desires of women. Sand suggests that Emilien's revolutionary gender politics do not come easily by having him enroll in the French revolutionary army without saying goodbye to Nanon for fear of revealing his love and not having the courage to leave. Symbolically, it is the old peasant Dumont who has lived with them who reveals to Nanon that Emilien loves her but that he is"jeune et pur, mais il est homme et il ne lui a pas été facile de vivre près de toi, confiante et dévouée en te laissant croire qu'il était aussi calme que toi/he is young and pure, but he is a man and it hasn't been easy for him to live near you, so trusting and devoted, and to let you think that he was as peaceful as you are"(176). Dumont's revelations upset Nanon who interprets Emilien's love as proof that he wanted to make her his mistress, then stun her when she realizes that Emilien wants to marry her, which she cannot imagine because of social differences. When Dumont points out that the Revolution has dismantled the class system and that the only future Emilien has is as a peasant, Nanon's objections are removed and she decides that, while Emilien is earning his citizenship in the war, she will become worthy of him by buying land. It is significant that Dumont is the one who finally voices Emilien's love and who articulates the consequense of the revolution because he is no threat to Nanon's demand for equality and autonomy: he is a peasant like her. He is an old man (with no sexual demands), and she has helped him as much as he has helped her.

By pointing out differences in the intensity of Emilien's desire and Nanon's refusal of desire, and linking them to their acceptance or lack of acceptance of social prejudices, Sand shows how embedded in social structures sexual desires are. Nanon, like most of Sand's earlier heroines, has no desire because desiring is inconceivable within a class system that denies her autonomy and equality. Confirming Mary Poovey's argument about Victorians's construction of female desire, Sand does not offer a woman-centered definition of female sexuality because female sexuality is a "critical place in men's contests for power and in women's social oppression"(30). Thus, it is only when Nanon is assured that her relation with Emilien is both socially acceptable and an equal reciprocal relation that she expresses her feelings.

Sand stresses the links between oppression and desire by providing a dramatic context for Nanon's expression of love and desire near the end of the novel. She is reunited with Emilien who is back from the war. When they embrace, she discovers that he has lost his right arm:

> A l'idée de ce qu'il avait dû souffrir, de ce qu'il souffrait peut-être encore, j'eus un violent chagrin, comme si on me   l'eût rendu à moitié mort. Je n'avais plus aucune pudeur, je le couvrais de caresses et de larmes et je criais comme une folle: Assez de cette guerre, assez de malheurs! Vous ne partirez plus, je ne veux pas!/At the thought of what he must have suffered, of what he was perhaps still suffering, I felt a violent grief, as if they had given him back to me half dead. I had no modesty left, I covered him with hugs, kisses, and tears and I screamed like a madwoman: Enough with the war, enough misfortunes! You won't leave again, I don't want you to! (221)

Her love and desire for Emilien, and her concern for him are expressed negatively: she voices her rejection of the public sphere (war is perhaps the ultimate example of the violence and power struggle expressed in the masculine public sphere), and reclaims Emilien for a private space. Although Emilien's amputation has been interpreted as the symbolic loss of his social privileges (Schor 154), I would argue that what is symbolizes is the mutilation that a patriarchal public arena (be it reactionary or revolutionary) operates on its participants, and is an indirect criticism of Emilien's attempt to abandon his nobility and gain legitimacy through action in a public arena, rather than being satisfied with action within the private sphere. For, to lose a right arm is to lose the possibility of becoming the peasant he wants to become. A peasant earns his living with physical labor, and when there is no hand, there is no labor. Thus, if it weren't for Nanon, Emilien would have to remain a failed aristocrat, which he acknowledges in the strongest of terms "Tu m'as sauvé de l'abjection...je t'appartiens/You saved me from abjection...I am yours"(227).

The loss of Emilien's arm signifies the impossibility to change alone one's position within a culture; Emilien needs the complementarity and partnership of Nanon, a partnership that Sand's earlier heroines never found. In the end, Sand refuses to reinscribe in the couple Emilien/Nanon the sexual and social differences that defeated her characters in other novels. Emilien and Nanon are both feminine and masculine, and the difference of the anatomy is dismissed; they are both "déclassés" (socially displaced). Because of their acquired education and their access to wealth, they are neither aristocrats or peasants.

In a letter to Flaubert she wrote a few years before *Nanon*, Sand expressed her views of sexual difference:

> there is this for those strong in anatomy: *there is only one sex.* A man and a woman are so entirely the same thing, that one hardly understands the mass of distinctions and of subtle reasons with which society is nourished concerning this subject. I have observed the infancy and development of my son and my daughter. My son was myself, therefore much more woman, than my daughter, who was an imperfect man (Letter XLIV, 15 January 1867, p. 49).

With *Nanon*, Sand demonstrated that there is only one sex and only one class. *Nanon* is her ultimate description of the cultural processes through which sex is created and transformed into gender, and of the social processes through which human beings are disenfranchised.

Unlike her previous novels in which cultural forces destroyed or silenced women who attempted to separate anatomy from a fate of victimization and dependency, either because they relied on Romantic male figures for their salvation, or because they could not escape patriarchal constructions of femininity, or even simply because they could not find any allies, *Nanon* represents characters who succeed and escape social and sexual essentializing.

NOTES

1. Her last novel was *Albine Fiore*, an unfinished epistolary novel about a dancer.

2. It became better known after the new edition by Nicole Mozet, and articles by Rogers, and Massardier-Kenney.

3. For a history of the separation of the spheres, see Joan Landers.

4. In fact, although not well-known by historians who tend to rely on the works of standard authors such as Balzac and Flaubert, *Nanon* is an extremely rich text for historical analysis and demonstrates Sand's precise knowledge of historical facts and her uncanny understanding of historical mechanisms. Although Mozet rightly points out that Sand rejects the violence of the Terror, we must not forget that, at the same time, she presents the reasons for the revolutionary excesses through the character of the terrorist Costejoux and her analysis is quite close to that of modern historians. See for instance, Peter McPhee's *Social History of France 1780-1880*.

5. For a summary of the social consequences of the Revolution and the image of woman developed under Napoleon, see McPhee.

6. In this regard, Sand differs greatly from the male nineteenth-century novelists who, as Eléonore Roy-Reverzy argues in *La Mort d'Eros*, strove to take woman back to her natural body and to her role as mother. Although, based on her analysis of *Jeanne*, Roy-Reverzy states that Sand equates woman and nature, here Sand challenges the naturalness of the body, and brings attention to the problematic notion of nature.

7. Apart from *Césarine Dietrich* (1870), *Nanon* is the only novel in which the first person narrator is a woman.

8. In this regard, Sand follows the pattern of Romantic works that have a remarkable number of orphans, as Allan Pasco has observed in his study of the Romantic age, *Sick Heroes*. However, whereas Pasco attributes this pattern to a widespread feeling of abandonment (61), in Sand orphanhood can be a blessing in disguise.

9. Sand's depiction of the role of women in the peasantry is accurate. Historical studies have shown that in the French peasantry there was a division of labor in which both men and women contributed.

10. The removal of older male figures here is in contrast with what happened in *Gabriel* where the presence of the grand-father is ultimately what causes the heroine's death.

11. See in particular his *Fraternité et Révolution française* (1987), and *Le Printemps de la Fraternité: Genèse et Vicissitudes* (1992).

12. See also David Pinkney's *Decisive Years in France 1840-47* who demonstrates that the revolution left intact fundamental aspects of French life, including social and symbolic structures.

13. For a chilling fictional representation of the consequences of aristocratic practices in the eighteenth century for relations between mothers and daughters, see *La Nuit La Neige* by Claude Pujade-Renaud.

14. One of them Pamphile even joins the Terrorists and pursues his former brothers.

15. See, for instance, Peter Dayan's comments in *Lautréamont et Sand*.

16. Costejoux's attempt to account for Nanon as a person who does not fit traditional sexual binary opposition echoes what Flaubert had told Sand on several occasions. For instance, "Under what star were you born, pray, to unite in your person such diverse qualities, so numerous and so rare?" (Letter XXVI, November 1866, p. 23), "what idea have you of women, O, you who are of the third sex"(Letter XCI, September 1868, p. 103), or "What a splendid woman you are and what a splendid man! To say nothing of all the other things" (Letter XXXVIII, December 1869, p. 148).

17. Nanon is quick to point out that his mother is also an exception but that is not sufficient to make him revise his views of the inferiority of women (188).

18. In "Féminité et espace public chez George Sand" Michèle Hecquet has nicely described Sand's reluctance to enter public space after 1848, and is right to argue that Sand's refusal to play a public role (for instance when it was proposed that women be allowed at the *Académie française*)stems, not from a devalorization of women, but from mistrust of such public institutions. It is interesting to note that Sand advocated women's civil rights (which would be exercised at a personal level).

CONCLUSION

It is symptomatic that, in spite of its seemingly romantic plot, Sand's last novel is the antithesis of French late-Romantic fictions as Margaret Waller has described them. Rather than expressing the expected male anxiety about the loss of old certainties about sexual difference (Waller: 176), *Nanon* articulates Sand's hope that denaturalizing sexual difference and laying bare the cultural mechanisms that turn sexual differences into social inequalities will free both men and women.

By finally feeling free to abandon a male narrator (and thus to position, from the start, woman as a subject rather than the object of male discourse and gaze), Sand's many representations of gender attain their strongest expression. Unlike the Sandian heroines that the preceding chapters described, Nanon unsettles the patriarchal order without anxiety and penalty. Unsurprisingly, Sand uses the French Revolution as the backdrop for her characters's successful gender negotiations because only a traumatic and disruptive event like a revolution or a war can provide the context for the gender changes she represents (an astute assessment of the situation of women in France if we recall that French women were given the right to vote only in 1944 near the end of World War II).

I began my introduction with a remark about Sand's obscurity and her dismissal as an innocuous writer of exquisite prose and pastoral settings. In this study of the representation of gender in her fiction, I hope to have showed that Sand's obscurity owes more to the valorization of the male *mal du siècle* in the French canon (and thus of the reassertion of male power in French culture) than to any weakness in her themes. The power of this canon is still such now that even as Sand is being constituted as a worthy subject of academic study, she is not treated equally, so to speak.

Yet, Sand's many representations of the mechanisms of gender construction and her rejection of hierarchical binary oppositions, her deconstruction of female women's internalization of patriarchal definitions of femininity, and her valorization of women characters as full human beings, may well explain why, although modern academics can deplore her lack of political involvement in feminist activism, nineteenth-century feminists considered her as an inspiration, from Eugénie Niboyet who nominated her as a candidate to the 1848 parliament to the radical Aubertine Auclert who kept a portrait of Sand in her apartment. It is not only that Sand's life was a model of sexual and social emancipation, but her works gave and continue to give her women readers a sense of empowerment. That Sand's achievement as a writer of gender has not been as recognized as it deserves is not surprising considering the slow development of gender studies within a French cultural context[1] and, until recently, the lack of interest in French women's stories and history.[2] Although her persona continues to attract attention especially in non-academic circles (one thinks in particular of French director Diane Kurys's new film "Les Enfants du siècle" about Sand and Musset, or the New York City play "Chère Maître" based on the Flaubert-Sand Correspondence), her fiction, which provides a major examination of the formation of gendered subjectivities, and which was immensely popular in the nineteenth-century, continues to be overlooked or taken lightly.[3] Sand's intervention on social reality in her fiction is minimized because she is not inscribed in the canon of French literary history, which privileges the masculine soul and the cult of beauty, form, and scarcity as expressed in the works of writers ranging from Balzac, Flaubert, Baudelaire, and others. However, the questioning of the formation of the canon, and the recognition by feminist scholars that symbolic struggles over social identities are as important as legal reforms[4] force us to reconsider Sand as a major figure whose tales of struggles in the private sphere constitute a central document not only in women's writing but also in the cultural history of the nineteenth-century.

NOTES

1. For a summary of the vicissitudes of feminist and gender studies in France, see Françoise Thébault's *Ecrire l'histoire des femmes*.

2. Reeditions and translations of works by important women writers such as Olympe de Gouges or even Claire de Duras have appeared only very recently, and significantly, in an American Context. See, for instance, Kadish and Massardier-Kenney's *Translating Slavery: Gender and Race in French Women's Writing 1783-1823*.

3. This kind of dismissal is beautifully demonstrated in the title of a positive review of "Chère Maître," the Broadway play based on the Sand/Flaubert correspondence. The title of the review is "His Ideas and Her Violets" (*New York Times*. 7 December 1998, sec. B: 5). Scholars are no better than journalists in this regard. Many feel free to make statements about nineteenth-century French literature without ever mentioning Sand's name; or some, who do make her the focus of their work, do so after reading a few of her well-known novels and some of her correspondence, a situation hardly imaginable in the case of other writers of her times.

4. For a discussion of the interrelation between linguistic and legal struggles, see Nancy Frazer's introduction to *Revaluing French Feminism*.

BIBLIOGRAPHY

Albertini, Pierre. *La France du 19 siècle*. Paris: Hachette, 1995.

Alcoff, Linda. "Cultural Feminism versus Post-Structuralism: The Identity Crisis in Feminist Theory." *Signs* 13.3 (1988) : 405-36.

Allen, James Smith. *Popular French Romanticism: Authors, Readers and Books in the Nineteenth-Century*. Syracuse: Syracuse University Press, 1981.

Alquier, Aline, ed. *Albine Fiori*. Tusson: Du Lérot, 1997.

Barrett, Michèle and Anne Phillips, eds. *Destabilizing Theory: Contemporary Feminist Debates*. Cambridge, UK: Polity Press, 1992.

Baym, Nina. "The Agony of Feminism: Why Feminist Theory is Necessary After All." *The Emperor Redressed: Critiquing Critical Theory*. Ed. Dwight Eddings. Tuscaloosa: University of Alabama Press, 1995. 101-17.

Bellanger, Claude, Jacques Godechot, Pierre Guiral and Fernand Terrou, eds. *Histoire générale de la presse française*. Paris: Presses Universitaires de France, 1969.

Bergman-Carton, Janis. *The Woman of Ideas in French Art*. New Haven: Yale University Press, 1995.

Bernstein, Samuel. *Auguste Blanqui and the Art of Insurrection*. London: Lawrence and Wishart, 1971.

Boose, Lynda. "The Father's House and Daughter in It." *Daughters and Fathers*. Ed. Lynda E. Boose and Betty S. Flowers. Baltimore: Johns Hopkins University Press, 1989. 19-74.

Bouchardeau, Huguette. *George Sand: La lune et les sabots*. Paris: Robert Laffont, 1990.

Braidotti, Rosi. *Patterns of Dissonance*. New York: Routledge, 1991.

—. Interview with Judith Butler. "Feminism by Any Other Name." *Differences* 6.2-3 (1994) : 27-61.

Bullough, Vern and Bonnie. *Cross Dressing, Sex, and Gender*. Philadelphia: University of Pennsylvania Press, 1993.

Butler, Judith. *Gender Trouble*. New York: Routledge, 1990.

Chalon, Jean. *Chère George Sand*. Paris: Flammarion, 1991.

Craft-Fairchild, Catherine. *Masquerade and Gender: Disguise and Female Identity in Eighteenth-Century Fictions by Women*. University Park: P.A.: Penn State Press, 1993.

Crecelius, Kathryn. *Family Romances*. Bloomington: Indiana University Press, 1987.

Dayan, Peter. *Lautréamont et Sand*. Amsterdam: Rodopi, 1997.

David, Maurice. *Fraternité et Révolution française*. Paris: Aubier, 1987.

—. *Le Printemps de la Fraternité: Genèse et Vicissitudes 1830-1851*. Paris: Aubier, 1992.

Didier, Béatrice, ed. *Indiana*. Paris: Gallimard (Folio) : 1984.

—, ed. *Lélia*. Grenoble: Glénat, 1987.

Ender, Evelyne. *Sexing the Mind: Nineteenth-Century Fictions of*

Hysteria. Ithaca: Cornell University Press, 1995.

Epstein, Julie, and Kristina Straub, eds. *Body Guards: The Cultural Politics of Gender Ambiguity*. New York: Routledge, 1991.

Erauso, Cataline de. *Lieutenant Nun: Memoir of a Basque Transvestite in the New World*. Boston: Beacon Press, 1996.

Erdman, David V., ed. *The Romantic Movement. A Selective and Critical Bibliography*. West Cornwall, Ct: Locust Hill Press, 1989.

Frank, Felicia Miller. *The Mechanical Song. Women, Voice, and the Artificial in Nineteenth-Century French Narrative*. Stanford: Stanford University Press, 1995.

Fraser, Nancy and Sandra Lee Bartky, eds. *Revaluing French Feminism*. Bloomington: Indiana University Press, 1992.

Garber, Marjorie. *Vested Interests. Cross-Dressing and Cultural Anxiety*. London: Routledge; New York: Harper, 1993.

Glasgow, Janice. Preface. *Gabriel*. Paris: Des Femmes, 1988. 8-22.

Godwin-Jones, Robert. *Romantic Vision: the Novels of George Sand*. Birmingham,   AL: Summa Publications, 1995.

Goreau, Angeline. "Review of Lieutenant Nun." *New York Times* 17 March. 1996: 28-29.

Harkness, Nigel. "Writing Under the Sign of Difference: The Conclusion of *Indiana*." *Forum for Modern Language Studies* 33.2 (1997) : 115-128.

Hecquet, Michèle. "Fémininité et espace public chez George Sand." *Femmes dans la Cité*. Ed. Alain Corbin, Jacqueline Lalouette, and Michèle Riot-Sarcey. Grâne: Créaphis, 1997. 333-346.

Hubert-Matthews, Veronica. "Gabriel ou la Pensée sandienne sur l'identité sexuelle." *George Sand Studies* 13 (1994) : 19-28.

Hunt, Lynn. *The Family Romance of the French Revolution*. Berkeley: University of California Press, 1992.

James, Henry. "George Sand." *French Writers*. New York: Library of

America, 1984. 702-09. Rpt. of "Letter from Paris: George
Sand." *New York Tribune* 22 July. 1876.

Jardine, Alice. "Introduction to Kristeva." *Signs* 7.1 (1981) : 5-12.

Kadish, Doris Y. *Politicizing Gender: Narrative Strategies in the
Aftermath of the French Revolution.* New Brunswick: Rutgers
University Press, 1991.

— and Françoise Massardier-Kenney, eds. *Translation Slavery: Gender
and Race in French Women's Writing, 1783-1823.* Kent: Kent
State University, 1994.

Keller, Evelyn Fox and Marianne Hirsch, eds. *Conflicts in Feminism.*
New York: Routledge, 1990.

Lanser, Susan S. "Toward a Feminist Narratology." *Style* 20.3 (1986):
341-363.

Laporte, Dominique. " L'Art romanesque et la pensée de George Sand
dans *Jacques* (1834)." *Études Littéraires* 29.2 (1996) : 123-36.

Laqueur, Thomas. *Making Sex. Body and Gender From the Greeks to
Freud.* Cambridge: Harvard University Press, 1990.

Lubin, Georges, ed. *Correspondance.* 25 vols. Paris: Garnier Frères,
1964-97.

Lukacher, Marilyne. *Maternal Fictions.* Durham: Duke University
Press, 1994.

Macherey, Pierre. *A quoi pense la littérature?* Paris: PUF, 1990.

Massardier-Kenney, Françoise. "Indiana: Lieux et personnages
féminins." *Nineteenth-Century French Studies* 19:1 (1990) :
65-71.

—. " A Question of Silence: George Sand's *Nanon*" *Nineteenth-
Century French Studies*   21 (1993): 357-65.

McCall, Anne E. "George Sand and the Genealogy of Terror." *L'Esprit
Créateur.* 35.4 (1995) : 38-48.

McKenzie, Aimee, trans. *The George Sand-Gustave Flaubert Letters.*
London: Duckworth and Co., 1922.

McPhee, Peter. *A Social History of France.* New York: Routledge:

1992.

Miller Nancy K., ed. *Subject to Change: Reading Feminist Writing.* NY: Columbia University Press, 1983.

Naginski, Isabelle Hoog. *Writing for Her Life.* New Brunswick: Rutgers University Press, 1991.

Overton, Bill. *The Novel of Female Adultery: Love and Gender in Continental European Fiction 1830 – 1900.* New York: St. Martin's Press, 1996.

Pasco, Allan H. *Sick Heroes: French Society and Literature in the Romantic Age, 1750-1850.* Exeter, U.K.: University of Exeter Press, 1997.

Perrot, Michelle. "The Family Triumphant." *History of Private Life.* Ed. Philippe Aries and Georges Duby. Cambridge Mass: Harvard University Press, 1987. 99-129.

Petrey, Sandy. "George and Georgina: Realist Gender in *Indiana.*" *Textuality and Sexuality: Reading Theories and Practices.* Ed. Judith Still and Michael Worton. Manchester: Manchester University Press, 1993. 133-47.

Planté, Christine. *La petite soeur de Balzac.* Paris: Seuil, 1989.

Ponsard, Francois. *Lucrèce.* Paris: Calmann Lévy, 1894.

Pontmartin, A. de. Rev. of *Lucrezia Floriani* by George Sand. *Revue des Deux Mondes.* Vol. XVIII. 1 April 1847.

Poovey, Mary. "Speaking of the Body: Mid-Victorian Constructions of Female Desire." *Body/Politics. Women and the Discourse of Science.* Ed. Mary Jacobus, Evelyn Fox Keller, and Sally Shuttleworth. London: Routledge, 1990. 29-46.

Powell, David A. *George Sand.* Boston: Twayne Publishers, 1990.

Rabine, Leslie. "George Sand and the Myth of Femininity." *Women & Literature.* 4.2 (1976): 2-17.

Rambeau, Marie-Paule. *Chopin dans la vie et l'oeuvre de George Sand.* Paris: Les Belles Lettres, 1985.

Reboul, Pierre, ed. *Lélia.* Paris: Garnier, 1960.

Reid, Roddey. *Families in Jeopardy: Regulating the Social Body in France 1750-1910.* Stanford: Stanford University Press, 1993.

Rogers, Nancy. "Sand's Peasant Heroines: From Victim to Entrepeneur, From "Connaissance" to "Idée," From *Jeanne* to *Nanon.*" *Nineteenth-Century French Studies* 24 (1996) : 347-60.

Roy-Reverzy, Eléonore. *La Mort d'Eros.* Paris: SEDES, 1997.

Rubin, Gayle. " The Traffic in Women. Notes on the Political Economy of Sex." *Toward an Anthropology of Women.* Ed. Rayna R. Reiter. New York: Monthly Review Press, 1975. 157–210.

Sagan, Dorian and Lynn Margulis. *The Origins of Sex: Three Billion Years of Genetic Recombination.* New Haven: Yale University Press, 1986.

Sagan, Dorian . "Why Women Aren't Men." *New York Times.* 21 June 1998, sec. 15: 1+.

Salomon, Pierre, ed. *Indiana.* Paris: Garnier, 1962.

—. *Née romancière: biographie de George Sand.* Grenoble: Glénat, 1993.

Sand, George. *Adriani.* 1854. Grenoble: Glénat, 1993.

—. *La Dernière Aldini.* 1837. *George Sand, vies d'artistes.* Ed. Marie-Madeleine Fragonard. Paris: Presses de la Cité (Collection Omnibus), 1992. 129-254.

—. *Gabriel.* 1840. Ed. Janice Glasgow. Paris: Des femmes, 1988.---.

—. *Horace.* 1841. *George Sand, vies d'artistes.* Ed. Marie-Madeleine Fragonard. Paris: Presses de la Cité (Collection Omnibus), 1992. 311-564.

—. *Indiana.* 1832. Ed. Béatrice Didier. Paris: Gallimard, 1984.

—. *Jacques.* 1834. *Romans 1830.* Ed. Marie-Madeleine Fragonard. Paris: Presses de la Cité (Collection Omnibus), 1991. 813-1026.

—. *Jeanne.* 1844. Ed. Simone Vierne. Grenoble: Glénat, 1993

—. *Lucrezia Floriani.* 1846. *George Sand, vies d'artistes.* Ed. Marie-Madeleine Fragonard. Paris: Presses de la Cité, 1992. 679-848.

—. *La mare au diable.* 1846. Paris: Gallimard, 1973.

—. *Mademoiselle la Quintinie.* 1863. Paris: Michel Lévy, 1863

—. *Nanon.* 1872. Ed. Nicole Mozet. Meylan: Editions de l'Aurore, 1987.

—. *La petite Fadette.* 1848. Paris: Garnier, 1981

—. *Story of My Life,* a group translation of *Histoire de ma vie,* ed. Thelma Jurgrau. Albany: State University of New York Press, 1991.

—. *Valvèdre.* Paris: Michel-Lévy, 1861.

Sand, Maurice. *Le Monde des Papillons.* Paris: J. Rothschild, 1867.

Schor, Naomi. *George Sand and Idealism.* New York: Columbia University Press, 1993.

Scott, Joan. *Only Paradoxes to Offer: French Feminists and the Rights of Man.* Cambridge: Harvard University Press, 1996.

Sedgwick, Eve Kosofsky. *Epistemology of the Closet.* Berkeley: University of California Press, 1990.

Simpkins, Scott. "They Do Men in Different Voices: Narrative Cross Dressing in Sand and Shelley." *Style* 26.3 (1992): 400-418.

Thébaud, Françoise. *Ecrire l'histoire des femmes.* Fontenay/Saint Cloud: ENS Editions, 1998.

Vareille, Kristina Wingard. *Socialité, sexualité et les impasses de l'histoire: l'évolution de la thèmatique sandienne d'Indiana à Mauprat.* Uppsala: Acta Universtatis Upsaliensis, 1987.

Vierne, Simone, ed. *Jeanne.* Grenoble: Glenat, 1986.

Waller, Margaret. *The Male Malady: Fictions of Impotence in the French Romantic Novel.* New Brunswick: Rutgers University Press, 1993.

Weil, Kari. *Androgyny and the Denial of Difference.* Charlottesville: University of Virginia Press, 1992.

Wernick, Robert. " A Woman Writ Large in Our History and Hearts."
    Smithsonian 27 (1996) : 122-136.
West, Candace and S. Fenstermaker. "Doing Difference." *Gender and
    Society* 9.1 (1995) : 8-37.
Willbern, David. "Filia Oedipi: Father and Daughter in Freudian
    Theory." *Daughters and Fathers*. Ed. Lynda E. Boose and
    Betty S. Flowers. 75-95.

INDEX

p.3. "Sand's use of narrators who are sympathetic
to the plight of female characters..."
[Contrast Francise Moserwald - M is A's victim
F is A's victim, too?]

FN
~~Perhaps~~ The Jewish element in Sand's early work
was of so little importance that one
simply used whatever stereotypes were available.
Since she was so sympathetic to most victim of
social, cultural, racial prejudice/abuse -- blacks,
native Americans -- one wonders at the exception,
there is a kind of evolution in her thinking by the
60's (Val + M, Syl) due to ~~Importance~~,
~~Change in relations with~~ lady personal friendships
w/ Jewish figures and changing attitudes in
French culture toward Jews + the Jewish question,
[reread chapter on 1860's in HIST of Jews in 19th C France]

— It would be interesting to examine Alida's strong
disgust for Moserwald from the gender point of view.

— p.11 — "destabilization of male narrative authority

FN p.125 FN#5 — Kenney claims that the stereotypes
used to describe M are deflated by the
positive ending of the novel. Not so! — It was
perhaps S's intention, but it ~~simply~~ as a
~~decuous~~ illusion.

FN
— p.105 — as FMK notes: "this could be language from
the author's preface" (not at all novelistic